MICROCREDIT AND WOMEN

MICROCREDIT AND WOMEN

By

Dr. M. Lakshmi Narasaiah
M.A., Ph.D.

Professor of Economics
Co-ordinator, Dept. of M.B.A. and Commerce
Special Officer
Sri Krishnadevaraya University Post-graduate Centre
Kurnool–518 002
Andhra Pradesh
(India)

DISCOVERY PUBLISHING HOUSE PVT. LTD.
NEW DELHI-110 002

First Published-2008
Reprinted: 2013
ISBN 978-81-8356-314-7

Published by:
DISCOVERY PUBLISHING HOUSE PVT. LTD.
4831/24, Ansari Road, Prahlad Street,
Darya Ganj, New Delhi-110002 (India)
Phone: 23279245 • Fax: 91-11-23253475
E-mail: dphbooks@rediffmail.com
dphtemp@indiatimes.com
Website: www.discoverypublishinghouse.com

Printed at
Dynamic Printers, Delhi

Preface

It is becoming more evident that the majority of the poor in developed and developing worlds are women. Poverty among rural women is growing faster than among rural men. Over the past 20 years, for example, the number of women in absolute poverty rose by 50 per cent as against some 30 per cent for rural men. The alarming evidence concerning the underlying trends for this process strongly indicates that the gender composition of the poor is veering towards a greater share of women.

Poverty manifests itself in many ways among migrant and refugee women, elderly women and children and indigenous women. Poverty is a complex, diverse and dynamic condition stemming out of depravation with respect to income, from social inferiority, isolation, physical weakness, powerlessness and humiliation.

Analysis of women's poverty suggest that its main causes stem from the perpetual disadvantage of women in terms of their position in the labour market, access to productive resources and income for the satisfaction of their basic needs. They also demonstrate that poor women possess exceptional resourcefulness, initiative and entrepreneurial spirit and that they show tenacity and self-sacrifice in trying to take a long-term view of their poor economic conditions and in safeguarding their livelihoods.

Dr. M. Lakshmi Narasaiah

Contents

CHAPTER 1

Women and Poverty

It is becoming more evident that the majority of the poor in developed and developing worlds are women. Poverty among rural women is growing faster than among rural men. Over the past 20 years, for example, the number of women in absolute poverty rose by 50 per cent as against some 30 per cent for rural men. The alarming evidence concerning the underlying trends for this process strongly indicates that the gender composition of the poor is veering towards a greater share of women.

Poverty manifests itself in many ways among migrant and refugee women, elderly women and children and indigenous women. Poverty is a complex, diverse and dynamic condition stemming out of depravation with respect to income, from social inferiority, isolation, physical weakness, powerlessness and humiliation.

Analysis of women's poverty suggest that its main causes stem from the perpetual disadvantage of women in terms of their position in the labour market, access to productive resources and income for the satisfaction of their basic needs. They also demonstrate that poor women possess exceptional resourcefulness, initiative and entrepreneurial spirit and that they show tenacity and self-sacrifice in trying to take a long-term view of their poor economic conditions and in safeguarding their livelihoods.

Development is the most important challenge facing the human race. The lack of progress in the last twenty years in the eradication of poverty and growing proportion of women among the poor is the single most important threat to the progress of development and its sustainability. As long as three-quarters of the world population continue to suffer from acute depravation, as long as profound imbalances in global consumption continue to persist, and, more important, as long as the spread of poverty, particularly among women, continues unchecked, there can be no development. The history of the development process shows again that the economic status of women is the key variable in the solution to the poverty crisis. It is time for the full recognition of the fact that women are part of the solution to poverty and to the stagnating development, not part of the problem.

The Earth Summit in Rio, the Human Rights Conference in Vienna, the Population Conference in Cairo and the Beijing Conference all were milestone events in terms of advancing our understanding of the crucial role of women in development and focusing the attention of the international community on the issues concerning the role of women in the work place and in society. All of them drew attention to women's full and effective participation in development. None, however, full articulated how to achieve this challenging task.

It is important to retain focus on the issue of economic potential when discussing poverty among women because it is clear that power is only meaning something in practical terms if it is reinforced by economic power. Women have the means to transform productive resources into such power if only enabling environment is created. It is not the lack of capabilities, but that of resources, which is clearly responsible for women's poverty.

Sometimes the so badly needed resources are not even truly scarce. Billions have been wasted on arms purchases around the globe and particularly in the countries, which cannot afford such misallocation of public funds. At the same time, women's organisations from grassroots to the international level are poorly funded. Such misallocation of resources at the time when poverty among women is increasing, is immoral and unacceptable, not only on the part of the governments which pursue such wasteful policies, but also on the part of the suppliers, who in most cases are developed economies.

Government's responsibilities do not end here. It is extremely important, and indeed it is the main duty of every government around the world, to provide a conducive environment for economic growth and stability by pursuing responsible and sound macro-economic policies, which will enable the economy to grow without marginalizing women. When inflation is rampant, when political climate is unstable, leading to conflicts and civil strife, little can be done for poverty alleviation.

CHAPTER 2

Lightening the Load for Women

Not only do women in India suffer greater poverty than men, they often have little choice but to pass it on to the next generation. Investing in women, therefore, is an effective way of building a better economic future for the poor.

Research findings from all sources are confirming what development practitioners have long observed: women are generally worse off economically than men, and the consequences of their poverty are more serious for future generations.

Women's poverty differs from that of men both in degree and in kind: women experience greater poverty and transmit their disadvantage more readily to their children, thus perpetuating the poverty cycle. At the same time, however, they are better able than men to protect children from the consequences of poverty.

It is this close connection between women's and children's fortunes that makes women's poverty a prime target for enlightened development practice. Anti-poverty policies need to reach poor women both to maximise social return on development investments and minimise the poverty of this and the next generation.

Breaking the Poverty Cycle

Poor women's rising participation in the world of paid work, however, does not necessarily guarantee a destiny of poverty. On the contrary, their earnings can protect children from poverty. Until fairly recently, the prevailing assumption was that any positive income effect of women's employment on children's health and well-being would be offset by negative effects of reduced childcare time by working mothers or by the substitution of older siblings in childcare. Recent studies, however, indicate a positive effect of women's employment on child health and nutrition. Women prefer to invest meagre earnings on child well-being and underscore the point that the income poor women earn can yield higher social benefits than income earned by men.

These positive effects of poor women's income-earning activities are not necessarily contradictory with the negative effects of women's increased work on their daughter's educational opportunities. It is likely that women need a minimum level of income to act on their preference to invest scarce resources on child well-being, below which their additional work perpetuates rather than halts poverty.

Policy and Research Implications

It is therefore desirable to implement policies that reinforce the virtuous cycle between women's and children's well-being that can occur in poor families when women have more income, and avoid those that can instead trigger a vicious cycle of deprivation between mothers and children. Circumstances which increase poor women's unpaid or very low-paid work can foster the perpetuation of disadvantage. These include the effects of declining household incomes during economic downturns, the decrease in service provision by the State which accompanies structural adjustment programmes, and many community and child-centred interventions that rely heavily on women's unpaid time. Anti-poverty packages need to reinforce poor women's roles as economic producers and avoid actions which increase women's unpaid labour for the promotion of family child welfare.

Projects which increase women's productivity in home and market production and expand their employment options can help turn the vicious cycle of poverty into a virtuous one. This necessitates executing agencies, which can work with women, in budget allocations to strengthen the capacity of institutions to implement and monitor gender-responsive employment programmes for the poor.

The reach of project interventions is restricted, however. Their impact is often short lived and while they can help to contain the cycle of poverty between mothers and children, they cannot in themselves transform women's economic activities. Changes in the policy environment are required for the latter. These include agricultural policies which target poor farmer and give women farmers access to land, credit and technical assistance; financial policies which promote the growth of small enterprises and foster entrepreneurship among women; and labour-intensive "pro-poor" economic growth policies. In addition, governments need to invest in upgrading women's occupational skills, and in a series of complementary measures, including overhauling social security systems, establishing gender-friendly regulatory frameworks for agricultural and industrial growth, and legislate on childcare options.

To guide these policies, we need: research that distinguishes families from households and seeks to understand the formation, structure and dynamics of families headed by women; longitudinal studies which provide a narrative for events in women's lives and assess the transmission of disadvantage between mothers and children; trend data which tracks changes in women's work as a result of changes in economic conditions and in implementation of economic and social policies; and analyses of the mechanics, costs and consequences of targeting interventions to female heads of households and poor women.

The policy-oriented research agenda is perhaps as ambitious as the policy agenda and both require funding. Investing in women should be an effective use of scarce development resources if these actions are guided by the basic principle of seeing women in India for what they are economic and social agents and not merely passive recipients of welfare.

CHAPTER 3
Fighting for Equality on All Fronts

In the wake of unemployment, global competition and deregulation, more and more women are joining an unforgiving job market. Are they in a position to exercise force against the discrimination they experience, and can they impose equality Of opportunity? To change things, women need to enter into combat on several fronts.

"For a long time, companies considered publicity to be a luxury and, in difficult times, the 'advertising and communications' budget was always the first to be slashed. Today, employers have become more aware that publicity has become a trump card in their strategy. Why can't a similar awareness become possible on the subject of women's employment?"

Financial problems and an evolution of mentality are the two core themes discussed in this paper on the Equality of Women in the world of work.

A Dual Observation

It is of a two-fold general observation: women are more increasingly joining the ranks of the active population: however, this trend is not matched by a parallel improvement in the quality of jobs to which they have access.

It is foreseen that women's rate of participation will be close to that of men by the year 200. In developing countries, the rate of women's activity is only 31 per cent on average, but this figure does not take into account the very large female participation in the informal sector and in agriculture. Thus, for example, in India, the adoption of a more general definition of "economic activity" pushed the participation of women from 13 to 88 per cent.

Women remained constrained in a relatively limited number of "feminine" sectors and occupations which are generally less well-paid and are less prestigious. During the last decade, however, an upward trend had emerged and more women are acceding to management and administrative posts and to specialized and technical professions. Moreover, an increasing number of women are setting up their own businesses. It can be noted, nonetheless, that very few salaried women are able to reach the higher echelons of responsibility due to the well-known "glass ceiling".

Among other disturbing observations is the increase in part-time work, which is especially prevalent among women with young children; other types of atypical work include temporary and occasional jobs, homework and subcontracting. Part-time workers are often young women who are less educated and less qualified than the average, which makes them more vulnerable. In Africa, in Asia and in Latin America, women are being called upon more and more to find work in the informal sector.

Even though some progress has been made in the area of wages, women's salaries are still between one-half and 80 per cent of those earned by men. Women's work is underestimated in most of the societies, and their income does not match their contribution to the economy. The difference in wages cannot be attributed to conditions of work alone. In the United States, in 1994 a woman in her twenties was likely to be earning 90 per cent of the rate of salary of her male counterpart.

Financial Problems

Financial problems and mentality issues emerged as two essential factors at every stage of the analysis of the causes of these persistent differences. The Fourm's participants' general consensus was that they should be tackled first of all.

Financial implications cannot be separated from the issue of women's employment, whether it is to justify its need or on the contrary to discourage it, or to explain the absence or lack of training of women who are available in the job market. Some examples are:

- In the countries in transition in Central and Eastern Europe companies underpressure to increase profits do not want to maintain social support services, which earlier had backed women's participation in the active population. These pressures are compelling women to leave the job market as the cost of childcare increases.
- In developing countries, especially in Asia, Africa and Latin America, the worsening of poverty and the increase in the number of sigle-parent families are requiring women to turn towards income-generating activities, but the lack of training and difficult access to credit constitute a major handicap.
- In Thailand, one of the major causes of young village girls resorting to prostitution is the state of poverty of their families, who are unable to afford secondary schooling for them.

Prejudices and Stereotypes

Several examples can also be found in the persisting traditions and stereotypes which are an obstacle in the path of women's march to equality of opportunity in the world of work.

- The Nordic countries, in particular Sweden, have instituted a parental leave which enables either one of the parents to take care of the young children at home; but it can be noted that very few fathers avail themselves of this opportunity.

- The status of a profession falls as the number of women entering it increases; salary levels thus become relatively less competitive. This trend is particularly clear in the teaching professions and in some medical professions.
- Measures of positive action are becoming more and more general. They cannot be successful unless they tackle discrimination on all fronts, together with the fixed ideas that are prevalent on the subject of the sexes. In fact, solutions to the financial problems that women's work causes are themselves going through an evolution in mentalities.

In a highly competitive job market, opportunities available to women are conditioned by the comparative cost of women's labour, as it is perceived by the employer. By virtue of the legislation in force in the majority of countries, the obligations linked to maternity protection and family responsibilities tend to, increase the direct costs of women workers; generally, employers bridge this gap by lowering the wages of women or limiting recruitment to childless women. This form of discrimination can also go as far as requiring medical certificates to guarantee sterility.

A Global Programme

To avoid such tendencies, efforts should be channelled toward two fronts. First, evaluating the relationship between a real cost-benefit (including the criterion of effective productivity) with a view toward eliminating the false idea that women workers are more expensive.

Secondly, making sure that in legislation, in practice and especially in the mentality of men and women all around the reproductive function and care of persons are recognized as social functions whose costs should be footed by society as a whole.

Recognizing the universal nature of the problem and the various fronts where one would need to enter into combat, this programme should aim at changing the relationship of power between men and women. For this change to become permanent, it will be necessary to consolidate the ground gained as the process continues.

Remedies should be composed of measures touching upon, among other areas, legislation and its control, access to jobs, to training and to resources, the reconciling of professional activities with family responsibility, outreach measures to groups of underprivileged women, improvement of information and research, the participation of women in decision-making and the mobilisation of public opinion.

CHAPTER 4

Women in Politics
Breaking Through the Barriers

The participation of women in political life is today on the agendas of most political parties in India. However, attempts to translate this goal into concrete reality have had limited success. A basic reason for this is the lack of conceptual clarity about the genuine commitment to the issue. For any such endeavour to be successful, it must be recognised that the equal participation of women and men in decision-making in all spheres is a prerequisite for effective democracy.

Participation means more than female membership in political parties, female voter turnout in elections or a token female presence in political bodies. Participation must be meaningful and effective, and must include representation in the political arena. This includes not only formal or higher level decision-making forums, but also other political units: the family, community groups, associations, trade unions and local bodies. These are crucial areas for intervention within which women can easily understand the issues and play an effective role.

The identification of barriers to women's political participation is obviously a prerequisite for overcoming them, but the visible barriers do not necessarily reflect the entire situation, and are often merely indicative of more deep-rooted problems. Governments tend to address the issue by devising measures capable of showing quick results. But tackling visible barriers without addressing their root causes results at best in temporary success.

Overcoming the barriers means not only eliminating them but also ensuring women's participation through other means. Affirmative action measures should not be perceived as privileges or concessions, but as interim measures to reverse existing imbalances, until such time as genuine equality and parity is achieved.

India must review its policies, constitution and legislation to see whether these have been discriminatory towards women, or have been ineffective in promoting women's rights. Since the issue of women's participation cannot be addressed in isolation; one must identify and assess factors affecting the development of a democratic culture or the recognition of human rights concerns. These factors include the country's political history, its socio-cultural, ethnic and religious diversity, the impact of traditional, customary, feudal and tribal laws, and the use of religious interpretations regarding women's rights.

One must review the prevalent general situation of women. While inequalities and imbalances exist in all places some have stronger patriarchal structures wherein gender roles are more rigidly assigned. It is particularly important to assess women's political participation, including political rights, participation in election process and political parties, representation in legislative bodies and local councils, women in the civil service and in trade unions, and women's groups and lobbies.

Barriers to women's political participation can be legal, social, financial or political. In addition to identifying such barriers, it is useful to assess initiatives taken by governments and non-governmental organisations (NGOs), to evaluate successes and failures, identify the reasons and make modifications.

Based on the above, appropriate multi-pronged strategies and actions must be devised. It is important to develop a clear policy articulating the effective involving of women in the formulation of laws and policies which govern their lives.

Measures must be taken to ensure the principle of equality as a fundamental right. National legislation must be amended or repealed to remove any discriminatory provision. Positive legislation must be introduced to promote or protect affirmative action measures. The language of the law must clearly address itself to men and women, changing the practice of using the legal 'he' to include 'she'.

Research must be undertaken to cover information gaps. Monitoring mechanisms, guidelines and indicators must be devised and a process of periodic data collection established, to assess changing trends. Documentation and analysis of innovative initiatives must be ongoing, to help in devising and modifying strategies.

Women's human rights and power sharing issues must be integrated in all training programmes of government, semi-government and autonomous institutions. Key personnel involved in decision-making and implementation need to be made sensitive to gender issues. Political education and training programmes for women are needed at the community level, for NGOs and community-based organisations, communicators, development workers and media personnel, etc.

Campaigns to change attitudes and social norms and project a positive image of women can be run through educational efforts and the media, and public discussions and debates. A clear stand should be taken against any misrepresentation of religion which stands in the way of women's equality and political participation.

Workshops and seminars should promote closer interaction between women in NGOs, advocacy and research groups, government departments, political leadership, trade unions, worker's associations and the media.

A minimum quota should be established for women in all sectors and grades of the civil service, including government, semi-government and autonomous organisations. A minimum percentage of key advisory positions, directorships, etc. should be reserved for women. Advertisements for government jobs should specifically state women's eligibility.

Electoral rolls should be systematically updated to include all eligible women. Education should be provided on electoral rights, political parties, election issues and concrete ways of holding candidates and political parties accountable. Political parties should publish their positions on women's rights issues, and encourage women to vote on issues that concern them. Constitutions of political parties should exclude provisions which condone or justify discrimination.

An adequate minimum representation of women in legislative bodies and local councils can be ensured by reserving seats through such means as putting women's names in priority positions on lists, providing financial support to female candidates, and making legal provisions that only those parties which give certain minimum number of tickets to women are eligible to contest elections.

A government ministry with the requisite authority should be designated as a focal point for devising policy, ensuring implementation and coordinating with other ministries and agencies.

An autonomous Permanent Commission on the Status of Women should be set up to function as a think tank on women's issues, to commission policy research and to review, recommend and monitor the implementation of policies and programmes in the field of development, rights and political participation. The Commission should comprise government representatives, NGOs, human rights organisations and experts in different areas.

A judicial authority should expedite women's human rights cases; this could take the form of a human rights bench, a tribunal or an equality ombudsman. These are only some of the basic principles and guidelines that can be adopted. Ultimately, however, no strategy can be effective unless it is also backed by the requisite political will and impetus.

CHAPTER 5

Equal Opportunities for Women in the Community

Over half the people in the Indian community are women. The change in women's contribution to society is one of the most striking phenomena of the late twentieth century. But although they have had the law behind them, women have yet to enjoy the equality they are entitled to in theory. Men need to contribute more to family life, while women have yet to make a real impact on decisions affecting the lives of everybody.

Technological advances have meant the decline of employment in manufacturing, and the growing dominance of service industries. This has meant more jobs for women, but not necessarily better working conditions. Most women are still in lower-paid jobs, and most still work mainly with other women in similar jobs and fields. Women are still under-represented in many sectors of industry, the professions and public service.

More and more women are involved in paid work. There is no job they cannot do, and they are entitled to equal pay for equal work, as well as the same terms and conditions at work, and the same opportunities for promotion. Giving women the opportunity to realise their potential in all spheres of society is increasingly important, for only by involving both sexes to the full can we develop human resources on really democratic lines.

Equal Pay, Equal Opportunities

The right to equal pay for equal work without discrimination based on sex has to be set out. Equal treatment in access to employment, training, promotion and working conditions has to be encouraged. Equal treatment in social security, as well as for the self-employed are very much needed. Rights to maternity leave and pay, and a guarantee of adequate health and safety at work for pregnant women and nursing mothers are urgent. The government has to encourage good practice on: Positive action, vocational training, childcare, combating unemployment, equal opportunities in schools, integrating women into working life, combating unwanted sexual behaviour at work, education, and updating protective legislation affecting women.There is still a great deal to be done before we can claim women in the community really get a fair deal and a chance to show what they can do.

Women are still often segregated into jobs that are less well-paid than those typically taken by men. They are often well qualified than men, and the jobs they do are often less secure. These are the kinds of inequalities the society must continue to combat and it will do so, as one of the ways of making sure women do not bear the brunt. Quality and quantity in women's employment is very important.

Better Opportunities to Earn a Living

Getting more women into paid work by promoting job opportunities, entrepreneurship and local employment should be the aim. The aim should be to help them fulfil their potential through better education, training and positive action. Upgrading their skills and equipping them with hi-tech know-how is a priority. Another major concern is helping parents juggle work and caring responsibilities via better services and terms of employment.

Getting Women in Positions of Power

It is hard to believe over half the community's population is female, given how little direct influence women have over what happens in our society. In an electoral constituency where half the voters are women, and where concerns for education, family health and food are paramount, both contestants up for election are male, and they speak to a largely male audience. The women, who work long hours and worry and sacrifice for their families and homes, fuss with the tea, hush the children up are on the periphery. If they are there at all. Polictics is 'men's business'.

Training to Keep up with the Times

Women need training if they are to benefit from growth and technological development. A network of training schemes have to be set up to develop training for women, to publicise their needs, promote information exchanges and encourage the involvement of employers and trade unions.

Changing Minds in School

There is no job women cannot do. A working party is looking at ways of encouraging boys and girls to range more widely in the subjects they take in school. It should aim to support teachers trying to avoid reproducing anachronistic stereotypes.

Pregnant women, mothers of new-born babies and nursing mothers should have the peace of mind of knowing they have secure health and social rights. For women who already have to combine their professional life with running a home and looking after children, political activity requires considerable sacrifice. Woman would be more ready to take them on if they thought they stood a chance of recognition on a par with men. That is far from being the case. If equal opportunities for women are provided definitely the country will develop at faster rate.

CHAPTER 6

Promotion of Women

Women made up more population, than half the world's population, produced 80 per cent of its food, laboured for two-thirds of its working hours, were paid 10 per cent of its income and owned one per cent of its property.

These figures conceal manifold forms of the disadvantaging and discrimination of women. Such as the Unjust division of burdens in families, the economic exploitation of women, the loss of their control over resources, and finally the unequal rating of paid and unpaid work. The latter, in the form of work for the family, on the land, for the community towards improving local living conditions, and nursing the old and the sick, adds up mostly to a 14 to 16 hour working day. True, employment of women has increased further everywhere in the world. But a number of them work in unsafe and socially unsecured conditions. They are also poorly paid and as a rule have hardly any chances to better themselves. Many women can earn money only in urban informal sectors or farming.

Global Public for Women

To be sure, the Decade of the woman (1976 to 1985), the adoption of the convention on eliminating every form of discrimination against women (1979), the key role of women in the development process and their rights have created a global public for them. Moreover, their activities have got underway a reorientation of international policies on women. But, despite numerous progressive international moves in the area of formal legislation, the political debates oil the legal status of women are in no way over.

Making general statements on the correlation of the impacts of social development and the situation of women is difficult because the political, economic and cultural framework conditions differ greatly from one country to another. However, discrimination against women manifests itself in most traditional as well as modern societies as a structural feature. Nowhere in the world are women treated "as good" as men, and all countries slip on the scale of human development when inequality between the sexes is measured. Differences between the life situations and opportunities of men and women still arise from unequal possibilities of access to employment, income, economic resources, health care, food, education and training.

Social developments such as fundamental changes in traditional family and social structures, migration, urbanisation, the contrast between traditional and "modern" ways of life, and often unfavourable economic developments for the majority of the people have a great influence on the role of the woman in the Various Third World countries. Moreover, the increasing differentiation of the south in terms of poorer and richer countries cannot obscure the fact that in the 1990s the general social conditions for the majority of women have not improved.

Almost one-third of all the people in the countries of the South live in life-threatening poverty, and the overwhelming majority of those are women. Female poverty has different aspects, such as poverty of income, low literacy, a lack of vocational training and the poverty of old age.

Further more, the continuing legal pluralism in many societies impedes efforts to achieve equality of status for women. Although in many countries men and women are meanwhile equal according to the constitution and legislation, there is still a great contradiction between constitutionally guaranteed rights and reality. According to religious law or custom, women in many countries are not equal to men. That means they have no property rights, or may not sign and contracts without their husbands' and constitutional rights, this implies the danger of becoming poor, particularly for single mothers, divorcees or widows.

Against this background it is no surprise that women are under-represented at political decision-taking levels, in government posts, political parties, trade unions and associations. The structures of many institutions give little support to women's interests, and managerial positions are held almost exclusively by men. In part, women-specific measures are seen as a compulsory exercise and, at best, tolerated as a fad.

New Opportunities

But in general the radical changes taking place in many countries open new opportunities for policies on women. On the one hand, this is because the extent of the disadvantaging and suppression of women is more visible. And on the other, because the fields of work for women have become wider—if mainly in urban centres. In some countries, women have been able to push through binding legal regulations (election laws, political party statutes, women's quota rules for local councils), in order to guarantee their stronger participation in parties and trade unions. With the programme slogans of "empowerment" and redistribution of power", women who are organized in self-help organisations, associations, networks and political parties are demanding participation in political decision processes and access to the political institutions. They are striving for social power in a bid to influence the factors which cause discrimination against them.

The transition from authoritarian to democratic forms of government in a great number of countries have placed women's organisations in a changed environment. There are now countless bodies, and their combined clout is changing the status of women and helping to broaden their scope for social action. But in some countries women are still faced with considerable difficulties in themselves with formal status.

On account of progressive impoverishment, however, the women's newly-wonscope for action and shaping their lives is markedly cramped. Current developments such as religious fundamentalism or economic recession have inhibiting impacts on new approaches to policies on women, in part, one must speak of a "backlash". Even where the legal position of women have been improved they have not been able to assert their social, economic and political rights. In some countries, it's feared that only elitist women's organisations will have a chance to break into the political process.

CHAPTER 7

Empowerment for Women?

The Gap Between Theory and Practice

Actually, the situation of women has changed completely in the last 30 years. At the beginning of the 1970s women were a blind spot in both development aid and the debate on it. The promotion of women is now established in all state institutions and non-governmental organisations (NGOs). Gender training is to sensitive development workers to take a genderspecific approach in analysing development processes, carrying out statistical surveys, and planning and evaluating activities.

From Integration to Empowerment

Those women who in the 1970s criticised development policy and its actors for being one-eyed must now see themselves as line-promoters and idea-providers. All the terms they used have been adopted in official usage. The image of the woman has changed from being a Cinderella-like, hard-done-by person, the poor soul, the victim, to a dynamic, reliable actor with apparently inexhaustible reserves of energy and creativity to bring to bear in a development process that has got stuck. The concept of empowerment has replaced the old "integration in development" approach in the promotion of women. And the women's approach (Gender and Development). This calls for the inclusion of men, taking a close look at the gender relationship and changing it into the long run.

All this undoubtedly progress which illuminates the blind spot. So is that enough to please women critics of the male-dominated development aid scene and female lobbyists for the promotion of women? Have they achieved what they wanted? That is, a policy on women which on the one hand takes up their practical, everyday needs, but on the other works strategically towards eliminating the hierarchy between the genders by structural changes? The fact is that one must differentiate between what governments, multilateral institutions and NGOs are saying and what they are doing.

Redistribution of Social Power and Control of Resources

The empowerment concept makes clear the political and economic gap between men and women, it aims at a redistribution of social power and control of resources in favour of women based on a development strategy which is no longer oriented on growth, the world market and military power.

The concept has had seemingly record acceptance in the executive suites and programmes of the governments while at the same time its substance has been drastically diluted. Taken on board hook-line-and-sinker by official policy, its politically critical teeth-namely posing the power question—have been extracted. It now has no bite critical of development and social policy. It just stands modestly and harmlessly for every strengthening and participation of women.

Professionalisation on the NGOs side and state orientation on the grassroots have brought activities nearer to one another. The modes of expression are identical. But where are women really at the centre of development practice? And where are they at the centre of developmental organisations? The promotion of women is still an appendage to development policy, including in most NGOs. That is shown not only by the low number of "pure" women's projects, but also by the subordinate role of women's interests and measures for women in integrated programmes. Defined as a "cross-sectoral task", the advancement of women is often reduced to the mere addition of a women competent. For example, in the form of small-scale loans for sewing machines. The few women in the organisations are assigned a low-ranking and sparsely-equipped niche.

Lack of Long-Term Strategy

The gender approach has made the yawning gap between rhetoric and practice even bigger. It might be useful as an instrument of analysis, if it is not debased to a technocratic checklist. But no-one at present knows for sure how it can be implemented. The international trend is to implement promotion of women less in "pure" women's projects than to integrate it in other activities. Parallel to that, there are signs of a trend in which the women's or gender sections of development agencies are being disbanded and integrated in country or specialist sections. Currently, however, there is apparently still a lack of concepts for implementing a strategically oriented advancement of women. If integration, or "mainstreaming", now takes place at the various levels, it is to be feared that the promotion of women will peter out rather than spread.

At the same time, disenchantment prevails among those who have understood that the advancement of women is a means to more rights and opportunities in life, more self-confidence and social recognition. The demand to effect structural change through projects founders on the general conditions. Like development assistance as a whole, raising the status of women is also in many regions becoming increasingly merely disaster relief and survival aid. All involved have long known there are no universally applicable formulas for projects, and still fewer handy "directions for use" for getting out of poverty arid blasting open patriarchal suppression.

The dilemma is clear. The economic crisis, the over-indebted and socially inactive governments, and the men who steal away from responsibility are saddling women with ever increasing burdens in securing survival. Thereby the women urgently need support. At the same time, the limited impacts of promotional measures, or even their boomerang effect, and becoming more obvious.

Many women are being catapulted into the exploitation mechanisms of the market and money economy only when they get involved in projects. Or, at least, the projects are speeding that of the projects the women neglect subsistence production and their traditional principles of the moral economy. But it is also clear that as a result of training programmes, new forms of organisation, development of new fields of action, and mobility, women's groups would collapse.

Thus, the old dilemma—of here a policy of small steps necessary for survival, and there big strategic and structural concepts—has got worse. But there's no way around it: the advancement of women must continue to seek bridges between being content with little arid the vision of a development that is more just to women.

CHAPTER 8

Population Growth and Women's Role in India

We have limited economic resources. There is a pressing need to abolish poverty. If population grows unchecked, abolition of poverty becomes very difficult. Due to the rise in population, illiteracy is growing as educational facilities are not expanding as fast as the population. Though employment facilities are being provided, we are not able to solve the unemployment problem. Though production and national income are rising, standard of living is not rising at the same rate. Thus growing population remains a serious drawback.

Conventional wisdom holds that slowing population growth is the key to solving a vast array of social, economic and environmental problems. To be sure, in a world of finite resources, unlimited growth in the number of people requiring food, shelter and work, not to mention access to natural resources, cannot be sustained. But the increasingly singular focus on demographics simply deflects attention from the fundamental social conditions—poverty, inequity, and the abject status of women—of which population growth is not the cause, but the consequence.

In India, as in much of the world, women are last in line for education, job training, credit, and sometimes even food—despite the fact that raising the status of women is the most effective way both to reduce birth and to achieve higher standards of health and economic productivity.

In India's tradition-bound society, where childbearing is often the only route to status and security, the majority of women have little to gain from having fewer children. The government, by contrast, is bent on cutting birthrates in half over the next decade, but has shown little commitment to meeting women's needs. And so a vicious cycle is perpetuated. As long as the status of women remains low, voluntary family planning efforts will continue to founder, tempting the government to use pressure to meet its demographic goals.

India will surpass China as the world's most populous country by the middle of the next century. Each day the number of people who lack access to adequate food, health care, housing, clean water and education spirals upward.

Female Education

Female education is the single most influential determinant of both lower birthrates and increasing empowerment for women.

Indian society manages to devote fewer resources to educating its girls than its boys. At the household level, cultural restrictions on female behaviour combined with the need for cheap household labour create a sharp gender gap in literacy. In both the Hindu and Moslem traditions, for example, notions of female "modesty" and "purity" dictate that unmarried females remain separate from unrelated males. Because the bulk of India's teachers are men, and most schools educate boys and girls under the same roof, many traditional families keep their daughters home, regardless of their income. Moreover, parents opt to invest in educating girls only when they perceive that long-term gains will outweigh immediate costs.

For the impoverished majority, the expense of sending a girl to school—paying for uniforms, books, and inhibitive especially when young girls are required to work at home and in the fields.

Women's lack of knowledge translates directly into poor nutrition and health for themselves and their offspring. In turn, these conditions causes high infant mortality—for which many women compensate by having more babies.

Nutrition and Health

Nutritional and health status is also marked by gender disparity. Both boys and girls in India are nutritionally disadvantaged, as nearly half of the country's households fail to provide even the minimum daily caloric requirements. But malnutrition is far more prevalent among females than males. From birth, male children consistently receive more and better food than their sisters, even though the nutritional needs of prepubescent boys and girls are virtually identical. Boys, given the same level of illness, are taken to doctors more often than girls. As a result of this neglect, far more girls than boys die in the critical period between infancy and age five.

Discrimination in feeding and health care produces one of India's most provocative signs of gender bias: In fact, the ratio of women to men in the country has been declining.

Women and Family Income

Son preference and the subsequently biased allocation of family resources is based on a series of myths the Indian government has failed to combat. One is the notion—not peculiar to India—that female do not contribute to family income. Throughout the world, women bear the "invisible" burden of unpaid domestic work and childbearing, the economic value of which is rarely reflected by official statistics.

Young girls in India generally work longer hours than boys of the same age. By age 10, girls in low income families are working eight or more hours a day assisting their mothers by tending siblings, collecting water and firewood, herding small animals, weeding fields, or facing the daily grind of low-paid child labour in the marketplace.

The poorer the family, the more vital the economic contribution that women and girls make, especially in the growing number of female-headed households.

Indifference Towards Women

The attempts to enhance agricultural productivity disproportionately benefit men.

Expansion of the irrigated area allocated to cash crops, such as groundnut and cotton, has come at the expense of food crops on which women depend to feed their families. And while the mechanisation of ploughing and levelling that comes with these projects reduces the traditional workload of men, that for women actually increases. Women still must carry out by hand the tasks of weeding, turning soil, and harvesting, but over much larger areas.

The result is to deepen women's poverty and enhance the perceived value of having many children to help with chores.

Not surprisingly, the share of married couples of reproductive age using contraceptives—now 40 per cent—is low, and most of these are holder couples who turned to sterilisation (counted as a form of contraceptive) only after having large families.

This bleak situation is shadowed by an ominous fact of history. Past attempts to reduce births in the absence of social changes enhancing women's status have been accompanied by increases in violence against females—in the beating and abandonment of women who don't bear sons, in female infanticide and child neglect, and in the rising use of abortion for sex selection.

Experience shows that even in India, with its immense tangle of troubles, well-designed programmes can produce dramatic improvements in family health while improving women's status and reducing births.

Increasing young girls' access to education and offering older women a chance for learning are essential to increasing female autonomy. Requisite steps include serious efforts to train and hire more female teachers, to set up literacy and tutoring campaigns in every state, and to encourage the growth of women's empowerment groups to foster changes at the village level. These strategies already have been proven in the southern state of Kerala, internationally lauded for its dramatic gains in the health and economic status of women and in slowing population growth.

Equally important are broad public education campaigns to raise awareness of the immense value of women's work and welfare to families and societies. The mass media also could be enlisted in the effort to change dramatically social perceptions of women's roles by depicting positive images of women and their economic contribution to society.

Much of the battle to win recognition of the importance of women's lives and health to societies will have to be fought by womon themselves. Indications are that women are responding to the challenge.

By filling the existing demand for quality voluntary family planning services, the government can make cuts in birthrates of at least 25 per cent over the next decade, thereby starting the process towards reducing the country's population. Equally critical to a long term-strategy of sustainable development is a sustained political commitment to improve the status of women throughout India. Only by working towards all these objectives simultaneously can the dreams of women for full partnership in society come true.

CHAPTER 9

On the Way to Commercial Microcredits

The Changing of a Development Instrument

The founding of financial institutions in the developing countries, whose target groups are supposed to be poorer people and, in particular, income-generating micro, small-scale and medium-sized enterprises, originated in the industrialised nations. Soon after Western "development policy" began in the 1950s and 1960s the donors noted that investment in infrastructure was insufficient to achieve growth. Reflecting on the experiences of Europe, state or mixed-enterprise development banks were founded in many developing countries with the support of various donors. The banks were to promote industrialisation as a substitution for imports, as well as farming, housing construction and regional development. Their common feature was that they combined the characteristics of a bank and a public authority. On the one hand, they managed loan holdings and handled payment transactions, and on the other they "prompted" development by non-repayable grants. Since these functions each followed a very different logic, the banks were required to undertake a difficult tightrope walk.

Exclusion of Small Borrowers

As a justification for the existence of state banks, even in liberal market economies people like to point out, and rightly so, that normal commercial banks would have scarcely any interest in the business of the "small fry" and, that they also shun longer-term financing of investment. A lender cannot beforehand tell the difference between good and less good borrowers, and must set a uniform interest rate for his credit offer. In order not to lose his cost-efficient and low risk customer's, meaning to avoid what the economists call "adverse selection", he sets the interest rate not as high as he would have to in covering his costs in the case of small borrowers, and "rations" his loans according to criteria such as reputation, collateral and business volume. Even in an otherwise completely liberalised model world, small borrowers, remain excluded from formal bank loans even if they would be able and prepared to bear cost-covering terms. That applies to an even because, other being equal, in most countries of the world they have lower incomes than men and also are discriminated against in access to property rights.

Therefore, in micro-economic terms, the idea behind the founding of development banks is well-founded. However, the design of the institutional structures, including the governance structure, requires a fine balancing of the bank and public authority functions in order to reconcile efficiency, cost-covering and the promotion mission. All too often, the easy way out for all involved is to combine the negative features of bank and public authority, meaning linking profit-mongering and the exclusion of small borrowers with a subsidy mentality and polarisation. As critical studies from the 1970s showed, following the initial euphoria, development banks seldom live up to their promises.

For the donor institutions, however, these banks are ideal counterparts absorbing financial and technical assistance. Thanks to their banking function in payment transactions, they practically never have outflow problems. In addition, they can at any time produce from their broad portfolios the projects demanded by a donor or; his client, such as parliamentary committee. And promoting development banks also promotes the exports of the donors, meaning the Industrialised nations.

And important point of criticism focuses on his "hidden" promotion of exports. This is that micro, small-scale and medium-size enterprises mostly do not need a great deal of imports, and especially not so long as they are still building a trusting relationship with their bank to overcome the asymmetrical information mentioned above. So they need loans in local rather than foreign currency.

When favourably-priced foreign currency; loans are available for projects which a bank public authority or company would in any case implement or promote, these can be used for other purposes, such as for imports of consumer goods or other agreeable things which otherwise could not be afforded. So who can blame politicians, bureaucrats, bank directors or companies when they prove to be fervent supporters of the financing of development banks!

Critics of the development bank system did not have an easy task in asserting themselves against the concerted interest of individuals on both the donor and recipient sides. But the search for alternatives began on a broad front in the 1980s.

Alternatives to Development Bank Promotion

Committed politicians, bureaucrats, academics, consultants and NGOs in various countries around the world began to get down to serious work in forming a new policy. Their efforts were based on the declared principles of poverty alleviation and sustainability in intuition-building in promoting micro, small-scale and medium scale enterprises via the finance sector. The results were published in the World Bank's World Development Report of 1989.

In an initial step, so-called "integrated" rural and urban projects and programmes were equipped with their own "rotation funds". Which were to finance employment and income-generating measures. However, due to their integration in projects focussed on infrastructure measures such as slum clearance, irrigation, electrification, public health services and regional planning, they degenerated typically into drawing funds for projects management's. That meant that a recipient mentality rather than a sustainable financial service provider structure came into being, and the mixing of loans and free gifts undermined rather than promoted a positive attitude towards market-conform financial relationships.

The Grameen Bank in Bangladesh is a special case. Here, the charismatic professor Muhammed Yunus persuaded the government to place a state bank in the service of poverty alleviation, and for landless women in particular. The results are not undisputed, especially since the bank is still very dependent upon subsidies. But this institution shows that participation in the monetary economy is anything but a matter of course, and that emancipation of women as free economic citizens is a goal to which purely technological financial principles should perhaps be subordinated. The Grameen Bank has yet to stand the test of developing into a sustainable institution without a heroic head and without subsides. Maybe it will really show now a poor country like Bangladesh can establish itself in the long-term as a "funnel" for permanent development assistance transfers. But a final assessment does not appear to be possible at present.

The NGOs are another alternative to customary development banks. Donors like to promote them because they are close to the target groups, or at least are able to portray themselves so. In practice, however, they prove to be problematical partners when it comes to develping a durable formal finance structure in the interests of small borrowers. As committed left-wingers, NGO members and leaders usually take a skeptical stance towards the market and its "bourgeois" laws. They are seldom willing to act as bankers with all necessary toughness and assume the "ownership" of a financial institution.

Critical evaluations show that in some case NGOs can be persuaded to found financial institutions and also run them as sole or co-owners. But the success of such upgrading projects depends very much upon the consultants and donors, and above all upon the existence of a capable leader. They cannot, however, be regarded as a norm.

The target groups and the academics advising them on-site noticed after a while, of course, that the big words were hollow. They realised that first and foremost it was matter of the hidden agenda of the national and international financiers and not particularly about reducing poverty among the target groups. If the "frontier" of the formal finance sector was to be pushed downwards in the direction of the poor, what they really needed in financial services had to be made available to them. These were small, readily available operating funds and emergency loans and secure and worthwhile investment options for temporary financial surpluses. Since poverty was a mass phenomenon, these financial products had to be offered with a loan technology, meaning a form of organisation, that gave them a mass reach with as much saturation as possible.

The then prevailing pattern was "controlled investment loan", involving obligatory consultancy, subsidised interest rates and relatively large sums to push through innovations in the context of "pilot projects" which, however, due to limited subsidy funds, never got beyond the promotion of a few "pilots". So the reforms diagnosis meant a radical change. But there were enough people on either side of the political "barricades" who became convinced by this plausible if hardy grandiose concept. As a self-supporting commercial system which nevertheless was in the interests of the target groups, it began to assert itself towards the end of the 1990s under the label of "commercial approach" or "new development finance".

After the Fall of the Berlin Wall

With the fading of utopic vision, empirically-based diagnoses gained ground and showed that precisely an unpretentious and reliable bank-customer relationship was the best contribution a bank could make to economic survival. In addition, they also demonstrated that in many cases a bank could in fact also help the target group of poor people, and particularly micro-and small-scale enterprises, to accumulate assets. Furthermore, it should be not only be mentioned but even emphasised that there were, and should be, public services of all kinds, including old age pensions, family allowance and similar transfers. Which counter poverty around the world. That was necessary to prevent micro credit programmes and similar bank services facing a demand they could not meet. Taking out a loan and servicing it with interest and repayment of the capital sum is always a burden for the borrower, and possible a benefit only in so far as it enable a special opportunity for profit to be sized. For the poorest of the poor, transfers are called for not loans and other bank or insurance services.

Development cooperation practicians on the ground and ideologically unbiased theorists alike came to these conclusions as early as the mid-1980s. But the ideological pressure did not ease until after the collapse of the East Bloc, when both the communist threat and the utopia of the non-capitalist workers' and farmers paradise disappeared.

So it is not surprising that shortly afterwards the patricians of both sides and the immediate representatives of the target groups got together with enlightened representatives of donors, consultants and academics to form an international coalition titled "New Development Finance". The Microcredit Summit of 1997 with Hillary

Clinton and already leaned in this direction, even if it still sent no clear signal in regard to the issue of dependency on subsidies. But the donors gave a green light for a massive financial promotion. World Bank president James Wolfensohn promised that together with all the other summit participants he would go all to ensure that by 2005 an additional 100 million families around the world would have microcredits.

The subsequent "Annual Conferences on New Development Finance", which took place at the University of Frankfurt – Main from 1997 to 1999, then developed into an important forum at which formerly diametrically opposed actors joined forces against the "ancient regime". According to their definition, "old" is everything which boils down to the demand of re-educating people and coupling loans with obligatory consultancy. In the long-term, that results in dependency on subsidies, becoming hostage to the political games of influential national rulers and donors, and loses sight of the declared target group of the urban and rural poor. All this applies mainly to smaller countries which receive heavy international assistance. In India, Pakistan and Brazil, not to mention China, the conditions have their own rhythms and special features.

After the end of communism there was a new situation not only in the developing countries and the North-South relationship, but also and above all in Eastern Europe. Established donor institutions such as USAID and the Reconstruction Loan Corporate (KfW) were supplemented by the multilateral European Bank for Reconstruction and Development (EBRD), and what were soon to be called "transformation Countries" lined up with the "classic" recipients of international development aid.

Internationally operating NGOs and consultancies with experience if the microcredit systems of developing countries were not also called for to assist the projects and programmes in Eastern Europe. The finance sector was perceived as the core of every market economy. At the same time, the donors soon recognised the importance of small to medium-sized business, trades, small holders and all the many disparate micro and small-scale enterprises for employment and the supply of the population. However, financial services were not available to any great degree to cover their needs.

It could now be seen that payment transactions did not function without commercial banks, and that this shortcoming and a considerable negative impact on small enterprises. Going beyond microcredits, which until then had always been the main instrument of financial assistance, the focus was now on deposits, transfers and all the other financial services that were important for the target groups. "Micro-financing" gradually became the generic term for the orientation of financial sector measures to benefit the "small people".

"Downscaling" or "Starting from Scratch"

By means of special loan programmes, which were kept separate from the other portfolios, the external donors sought at first to persuade the existing banks to downscale their activities and address the newly emerging small to medium-size business in the private sector. On balance, the result was rather meager, for these programmes did little to influence the characteristics of the major Eastern European commercial banks. And every time some of them were privatised or had to be shut down due to financial rows or corruption scandals, it affected the special small enterprises portfolios regardless of how efficiently they were managed.

Besides using this channel via the big banks, donors also began building up loan programmes through NGOs and local chambers of commerce. The result here were also disappointing, for local implementing organisations are mostly unsuitable for a substantial mass banking business.

But senior officials and executive at donors and consultancies soon had the idea of founding their own micro-finance institutes. "Starting from scratch" green field banking and similar terms began to make the rounds The first "Micro-Enterprises Bank" came into being in Bosnia and soon afterwards other micro-finance institutions (MFIs) were founded.

Unlike customary development cooperation projects, which have a timeframe, the MFIs are open-ended, and consultants in the North also see themselves as long-term partner. In contrast, international development organisations are more and more becoming second-class partners from which local bodies must sooner or later separate themselves again to avoid being left in the lurch. After all, their cooperation has a time limit, and they will leave the country again.

In view of the challenges of globalisation, the banks should perhaps consider using their development projects to establish a network of long term investments and thus fulfil their promotion mission in favour of the "Small people" not only locally and nationally, but also globally.

CHAPTER 10

Small People's Banks

The Role of Micro-Enterprise Banks in Development Assistance

Micro-enterprise banks (MEBs) grant many small loans, offer investment opportunities, and handle their customer's payment transactions at home and abroad. They are licensed by and under the control of local banking supervisory bodies. They are growing fast and expanding their branch networks.

Direct observation and simple arithmetics show that the banks make a substantial contribution to local finance systems and thus to their countries' economic development. Their input to development is socially relevant above all because they offer their services first and foremost to the kinds of customers in which existing local banks appear to have a no interest. Apart from the jobs in the small enterprises they finance, the banks themselves offer many young people skilled employment. In addition, these small banks make a profit. They also have private investors, who are becoming more and more important to them.

All that appears to be quite astonishing, most of all perhaps because MEB are founded as development assistance projects. A consensus has emerged in development cooperation in recent years in which institutions such as MEB appear to be a new model. The MEBs are the newcomers on this list, and their success can already be noted from their figures. A more precise analysis seeking to isolate the quantitative influence of their various success factors, including that of donor inputs, would require more data than is available due to the newness of the MEBs. But what already appears to be clear is that establishing new banks is a promising new approach in the micro-finance sector.

Learning from Experience

The new approach is an attempt to draw lessons from the positive and negative experiences of financing development and implement them. An initial and very positive lesson relates to the methods of granting loans. It is indeed possible to grant, with tolerable costs and a very low repayment default rate, microcredits to people whom conventional bankers view as not creditworthy and in whom established banks have no interest.

This methodology is neither a secret nor difficult to learn. However, it is not compatible with the organisational structures and processes of customary banks, which are focussed on other business fields and target groups. That is the second lesson, drawn from many so-called downscaling projects. To be successful at granting small-scale and micro-loans, a bank must be capable and willing to go in for far-reaching decentralisation of decision-making agree to performance related pay, and offer skilled employees credible job and promotion prospects. And to achieve that the bank must also grow. As a counterbalance to decentralisation bank staff must be very well trained and highly motivated, and sophisticated control mechanisms must be in place.

These considerations are good reasons for offering financial services for "small" people through special institutions. This was attempted in the past by the strategy of upgrading existing loan granting NGOs by external support. The experiences with upgrading were in part very good, but some of them were problematical.

The third lesson is clearly positive. It is indeed possible, with acceptable expenditure of development assistance funds to upgrade on existing institution and transform it into an efficient bank for "small" customers. And that brings us to the fourth and rather negative lesson. Upgrading as inherent limits. Positions based on power and self-interest arise in the process of developing and promoting existing institutions, and they obstruct a project's progress. The manager or founder/initiator of an externally promoted and relatively successful loan-granting NGO naturally has little interest in his or her institution becoming a "proper bank" for whose management they would not be suitable, if due only to the banking supervisory body's qualification requirements. The donors, too, who usually have financed the expansive first stage of an upgrading process, regrettably often do not see themselves as owners and advocates of the promoted institutions and, above all, of the target groups they have not yet reached. As a rule they are satisfied with what has been achieved. They avoid a confrontation with those who defend their positions and thereby impede further development of the institution, even if this is desirable in developmental terms.

It is precisely successful institution—strengthening that aggravates the dichotomy between those who have attained influential and prestigious positions and want to protect their interests and the interests of the target groups and the bank's employees in expanding the institution. This conflict, for which there is plenty of empirical proof, has a structural cause. NGOs have no owners that have an "objective" interest in the long-term financial and developmental success of the projects and will therefore assume a constructive role. Formalising the institution changes nothing so long as there is not at the same time a substantial change in the ownership structure.

Setting up New Micro-finance Banks

The new approach differs in two respects from customary institution building by upgrading. First, the phases of institution strengthening ahead of formalising and transforming are leapfrogged. Instead of expanding and converting an NGO, it is about setting up a new micro-finance bank. Second, the issue of ownership and governance are clarified from the start based on the perspective of medium-term development. But the more technical problems of granting loans and the design of the institution can be solved largely according to proven models.

Setting up a bank from scratch in a developing or transformation country involves a number of steps. The first is project identification. The main question here is whether the project could make developmental sense. The second step is to assess whether a new bank is really necessary and meaningful in developmental terms, economically sound and politically feasible, Economic soundness is assessed under the assumption that for the initial phase technical assistance and refinancing of the first loans on favourable terms can be procured. Without these, the projects could not be implemented at precisely the time when they appeared to be particularly important for development.

In the third step, provisional consensus must be reached among potential investors and the so-called sponsor, who is to build up the bank in technical terms and manage it during its early days. In addition, knock-on financing from one or more donors must be secured. What is decisive for potential inclusion as an international investor is first to be willing and able to play an active role as an owner and be present on the board of the new bank. The second requirement is to contribute to the success of the project above and beyond having a capital stake in it. The third condition is to share the concept of a commercially oriented strategy of institution building that is nevertheless committed to development.

The second condition can be fulfilled by, for example, an investor also functioning as a donor and providing Technical Cooperation funds or loans or procuring them from pure donors. If the other two conditions were not met, coordination would be too difficult. The group of possible investors who fulfill as the perquisites is very limited. Investors who had only capital to offer would be quite easy to find. But including them in the setting-up phase would only hamper coordination. In principle, the development institutions are possible project sponsors, who should also be investors. But in practice there is more a tendency to call in a private company with relevant experience.

The fourth step is to develop a business plan. This forms the basis for a biding commitment by the investors, the sponsors and, if applicable, the donors. The plan also covers the founding of a local company as the legal entity responsible for the future bank, the application for bank licence, and the technical preparation for opening the bank including recruiting and training local staff.

If the entire process is completed quickly, it takes a year. Based on experienced, compared with upgrading projects the time needed for setting up a functioning bank is shorter, the cost to donors lower and the chances of success greater.

Success Depends on Natural Trust and Experience

The success of the new banks promotes their employee's commitment and loyalty and strengthens the link between investors and sponsors. It thereby reinforce precisely the factors that are required of them to allow this success to occur. That is why time and gain the same actors get together in various projects as international investors, sponsors and donors. All parties must know each other well and have well-founded trust in each other for last and successful handling of the process. And only a rapid sequence of similar projects involving the same actors offers the opportunity of transferring knowledge, including qualified staff, from one "building site" to the next. Where if not in similar projects, can someone who is to set up and manage a microfinacne bank or their loans department learn how to do it? Where, other than in a "sister" project, is local staff to be trained before the bank is opened? Where, other than in similar and effectively linked banks, are there the opportunities of advancement, which must be offered, to the best local staff in order to strengthen their motivation and retain them?

CHAPTER 11

After the Microcredit Summit

How to Implement its Anti-Poverty Strategy

More than 2500 people from 100 countries gathered in Washington in February 1997, to participate in the Microcredit Summit. The goal of the organisers of the Summit is to reach 100 million poor families around the world with microcredits and other financial services within the next ten years. As there are at least six people in a family, 600 million people would benefit from access to micro finance. This means that half of the people in extreme poverty could have the opportunity to get out of their misery.

The fact that more than one billion people in the world are still living in extreme poverty is a sign of failure of our development policy and a scandal for human society. Now there is no longer any excuse. We have learned in the last years that microcredit is one of the best tools to eradicate poverty. At the Summit, there was a consensus between politicians, practitioners, donors, scientists and NGOs on how to reach this goal. Particular emphasis is given to strengthening poor people in their capacities. It is also understood that lack of funds is only one aspect of the most pressing problems in the field of micro-finance.

The Approach

The overall goal can be achieved by designing and establishing an appropriate and sustainable institutional framework on the national level in the developing countries. The most significant elements within a feasible strategy to achieve the goal are the following:

- Decentralised, bilateral fund-raising and financing under commonly accepted standards are preferred, whereas the creation of a new global facility as a supranational mobilising and channeling mechanism for microcredit should not be pursued.
- The focal point of the future strategy should be the creation and the support of independent and recipient countries which will operate under the basic principles of outreach. Moreover, the mobilisation of domestic funds will be of particular importance. Promoting agencies as wholesale institutions should identify and assess eligible microfinance institutions on the basis of a widely accepted set of performance criteria, identify institutional weakness and requirements at national level and execute programmes for the funding, institutional strengthening, training and linking of participating institutions.
- The NGO results, which helped organise the Microcredit Summit, will perform as a catalyst in creating public awareness regarding the crucial role of microfinance in poverty alleviation in donor as well as recipient countries.

The Consultative Group to Assist the Poorest (CGAP) will be responsible for the creation of promoting agencies at the national level. The role of CGAP will be the monitoring and coordinating of promotional activities. It will act as a platform for setting consistent standards for the operation of individual programmes.

The Next Steps

Under the guidance of CGAP, interested donor and recipient countries should immediately begin to discuss the institutional profiles of promoting agencies and performance criteria of participating institutions. Moreover, the necessary operational procedures for the functioning of the institutional framework at the whole sale level need to be defined by CGAP. CGAP should identify promoting agencies within the next six months. It will be responsible for the coordination of funding activities. Capacity building for promoting agencies as well as for recipient institutions will be a crucial issue. A pilot phase in a small number of countries should be designed to gain experience with the proposed institutional framework in order to develop it further and also determine the adequate volume of funding for potential recipient institutions. Bilateral donors should support these activities.

CHAPTER 12

A Rare and Precious Resource

Fresh water is a scarce commodity. Since it's impossible to increase supply, demand and waste must be reduced. But how?

Water is a bond between human beings and nature. It is ever-present in our daily lives and in our imaginations. Since the beginning of time, it has shaped extraordinary social institutions, and access of it has provoked many conflicts.

But most of the world's people, who have never gone short of water, take its availability for granted. Industrialists, farmers and ordinary consumers blithely go on wasting it. These days, though, supplies are diminishing while demand is soaring. Everyone knows that the time has come for attitudes to change.

Few people are aware of the true extent of fresh water scarcity. Many are fooled by the huge expanses of blue that feature on maps of the world. They do not know that 97.5 per cent of the planet's water is salty—and that most of the world's fresh water—the remaining 2.5 per cent—is unusable: 70 per cent of it is frozen in the icecaps of Antarctica and Greenland and almost all the rest exists in the form of soil humidity or in water tables which are too deep to be tapped. In all, barely one per cent of fresh water 0.007 per cent of all the water in the world, is easily accessible.

Over the past century, population growth and human activity have caused this precious resource to dwindle. Between 1900 and 1995, world demand for water increased more than six fold—compared with a threefold increase in world population. The ratio between the stock of fresh water and world population seems to show that in overall terms there is enough water to go round. But in the most vulnerable regions, an estimated 460 million people (8 per cent of the world's population) are short of water, and another quarter of the planet's inhabitants are heading for the same fate. Experts say that if nothing is done, two-thirds of humanity will suffer from a moderate to severe lack of water by the year 2025.

Inequalities in the availability of water—sometimes even within a single country—are reflected in huge difference in consumption levels.

Scarcity is just one part of the problem. Water quality is also declining alarmingly. In some areas, contamination levels are so high that water can no longer be used even for industrial purposes. There are many reasons for this untreated sewage, chemical waste, fuel leakages, dumped garbage, contamination of soil by chemicals used by farmers. The worldwide extent of such pollution is hard to assess because data are lacking for several countries. But some figures give an idea of the problem. It is thought for example that 90 per cent of waste water in developing countries is released without any kind of treatment.

Things are especially bad in cities, where water demand is exploding. For the first time in human history, there will soon be more people living in cities than in the countryside and so water consumption will continue to increase. Soaring urbanisation will sharpen the rivalry between the different kinds of water users.

Curbing the Explosion in Demand

Today, farming uses 69 per cent of the water consumed in the world, industry 23 per cent and households 8 per cent. In developing countries, agriculture uses as much as 80 per cent. The needs of city-dwellers, industry and tourists are expected to increase rapidly, at least as much as the need to produce more farm products to feed the planet. The problem of increasing water supply has long been seen as a technical one, calling for technical solutions such as building more dams and desalination plants. Wild ideas towing chunks of icebergs from the poles have even been mooted.

But today, technical solutions are reaching their limits, Economic and socio-ecological arguments are levelled against building new dams, for example: dams are costing more and more because the best sites have already been used, and they take millions of people out of their environment and upset ecosystems. As a result, twice as many dams were built on average between 1951 and 1977 than during the past decade.

Hydrologists and engineers have less and less room for manoeuvre, but a new consensus with new actors is taking shape. Since supply can no longer be expanded—or only at prohibitive cost for many countries—the explosion in demand must be curbed along with wasteful practices. An estimated 60 per cent of the water used in irrigation is lost through inefficient systems, for example.

Economists have plunged into the debate on water and made quite a few waves. To obtain "rational use" of water i.e. avoiding waste and maintaining quality, they say consumers must be made to pay for it. Out of the question, reply those in favour of free water, which some cultures regard as "a gift from heaven". And what about the poor, ask the champions of human rights and the right to water? Other important and prickly questions being asked by decision-makers are how to calculate the "real price" of water and who should organise its sale.

The State as Mediator

The principle of free water is being challenged. For many people, water has become a commodity to be bought and sold. But management of this shared resource cannot be left exclusively to market forces. Many elements of civil society—NGO's, researchers, community groups—are campaigning for the cultural and social aspects of water management to be taken into account.

Even the World Bank, the main advocate of water privatisation, is cautious on this point. It recognises the value of the partnerships between the public and private sectors which have sprung up in recent years. Only the state seems to be in a position to ensure that practices are fair and to mediate between the parties involved—consumer groups, private firms and public bodies. At any rate, water regulation and management systems need to be based on other than purely financial criteria. If they aren't, hundreds of millions of people will have no access to it.

CHAPTER 13

Action for Safe Motherhood

Countries vary enormously in terms of the situations and challenges they face and their capacity to address these. However, experience from around the world over the past decade has demonstrated that a number of features are common to successful efforts to address maternal mortality. Reducing maternal mortality requires coordinated, long-term efforts. Actions are needed within families and communities, in society as a whole, in health systems, and at the level of national legislation and policy. Further, interactions among the interventions in these areas are critical to reducing maternal mortality and to building and supporting momentum for change.

Legislative and Policy Actions

Changes in legislation and policy are essential to ensure safe motherhood. Long-term political commitment is an essential prerequisite. When decision-makers at the highest levels are resolved to address maternal mortality, the resources needed will be mobilized and the essential policy decisions will be taken. Without this level of commitment over the long-term, projects cannot become programmes and activities cannot be sustained.

A supportive social, economic, and legislative environment allows women to overcome the various obstacles that limit their access to health care, such as distance from their homes to appropriate health facilities, lack of transport and, more critically, financial and social barriers. Proper maternal health care is limited when women have to pay for services and essential drugs, and when they must bear substantial hidden costs such as time lost for housework, paid employment, food production, and childcare. Legislation that supports women's access to care must be formulated to permit health workers at the periphery of the health system to perform specific life-saving functions. Failing this, only highly skilled health professionals, based largely in urban centres, can provide such care, and only women with sufficient money and the means to reach such centres can benefit from it.

With these objectives, careful review of national laws and policies is necessary, particularly in the following areas:

- ***Family planning:*** Statutes that restrict women's access to family planning services (e.g. by requiring that a woman be married or that she should have her husband's approval) should be repealed. Policies must ensure that all couples and individuals have access to good-quality, voluntary, client-oriented, and confidential family planning information and to services that offer a wide choice of effective contraceptive methods. Policies should address regulatory, social, economic, and cultural factors that limit women's control over sexuality and reproduction, in order that pregnancies that are too early, too late, or too frequent may be avoided.

- ***Adolescents and children:*** Policies and programmes should encourage late marriage and child-bearing and an expansion of the economic and educational opportunities for girls and women. Promotion of good nutrition in childhood and adolescence, as well as supplementation if necessary during pregnancy, provides protection for both women and their future children. Policies should also enable adolescents to take responsibility for and protect their sexual and reproductive health, and facilitate their access to health information and services. All children, before they reach the age at which they become sexually active, need to be taught the risks of unprotected sex and helped to develop the skills needed to protect themselves from sexual coercion.

- ***Barriers to access:*** Assigning health workers trained in midwifery to village-based health facilities can help overcome problems of distance and transport. Health workers should also be trained to deal sympathetically with women patients. Policies should support the provision of services at minimum cost; at the same time, health workers should have job security, be paid adequate wages, and be provided with sufficient supplies to do their jobs. Policies that will increase women's decision-making power, particularly in regard to their own health, are also essential.

- ***Regulation of practice:*** Protocols and statutes aimed at providing both routine maternal care and referral facilities for obstetric complications at each level of the health system need to be developed. Responsibilities at each level for supervision, deployment of health care personnel, remuneration, and reporting procedures must be defined nationally. Development and promotion of education and training curricula are important, as is the setting of national norms and standards to govern the selection of trainees, trainers, and supervisors.

- ***Delegation of authority:*** Services should be decentralized so that facilities are available as close to people's homes as possible. Adequate supplies and equipment and trained staff should be available in all health facilities, particularly in rural and remote areas, together with written policies and protocols to guide service provision and to allow certain functions to be delegated to personnel at lower levels (when appropriately trained).

- ***Abortion:*** Availability of services for management of abortion complications and post-abortion care should be ensured by appropriate legislation. Where abortion is not prohibited by law, facilities for the safe termination of pregnancy should be made available. National policy can discourage unsafe abortion practices by promoting protection against unwanted pregnancy, and national helath campaigns to publicize the risks of unsafe abortion and the need to recognize and seek treatment for abortion complications.

CHAPTER 14

Safe Motherhood is a Human Rights Issue

The death of a woman during pregnancy or childbirth is not only a health issue but also a matter of social injustice. Of the human rights currently acknowledged in national constitutions and in regional and international human rights treaties, many can be applied to safe motherhood. Many such treaties and conventions are based on the 1948 Declaration of Human Rights; They include (1) the Convention on the Elimination of All Forms of Discrimination against Women, (2) the Convention on the Rights of the Child, (3) the European Convention for the Protection of Human Rights and Fundamental Freedoms, (4) the American Convention on Human Rights, and (5) the African Charter on Human and Peoples' Rights (6).

Human rights of relevance to safe motherhood can be grouped into the following four principal categories:

- ***Rights relating to life, liberty and security of the person,*** which require governments to ensure both access to appropriate health care during pregnancy and childbirth, and women's rights to decide whether, when, and how often to bear children. Governments must therefore address factors within the economic, legal, social and health systems that deny women these fundamental rights.

- ***Rights relating to the foundation of families and of family life,*** which require governments to provide access to health-services and other facilities that women need to establish families and to enjoy life within a family.
- ***Rights relating to health care and the benefits of scientific progress, including health information and education,*** which require governments to provide access to good sexual and reproductive health care with appropriate referral systems. The measures needed to ensure safe motherhood can be provided through primary health care irrespective of a country's level of economic development. Central to these rights is information on a range of reproductive health issues, including family planning, abortion and sex education.
- ***Rights relating to equality and non-discrimination,*** which require governments to provide access to services such as education and health care without discriminatory grounds such as sex, marital status, age and socio-economic class. Discriminatory policies include requirements for a woman to obtain the consent of her husband for particular health care interventions, requirements for parental authorisation which have a differential impact on girls, and laws that criminalise medical procedures that only women need. Governments are in violation of their obligations when they fail to implement laws that effectively protect women's interests or to allocate health resources to meet women's particular need for safe pregnancy and childbirth.

The actions that governments need to take to promote safe motherhood as a human right fall into three groups:

- ***Reform of laws*** that prevent women from attaining the highest possible levels of health and nutrition needed for safe pregnancy and childbirth and that inhibit access to reproductive health information and services such as laws requiring women in need of health care to seek the authorisation of husbands or other family members first.
- ***Implementation of laws*** that foster women's right to good health and nutrition and that protect women's health interests such as laws that prohibit child marriage, female genital mutilation, rape and sexual abuse. Every effort should be made to implement laws that encourage the healthy timing of births, such as those that support the education of girls, set a minimum age for marriage and ensure women's access to essential health care.
- ***Application of human rights*** in national legislation and policy to advance safe motherhood.

CHAPTER 15

An Agenda for Change

The world's growing population, combined with unsustainable production and consumption patterns, is putting increasing stress on air, land, water, energy, and other essential resources.

- Development strategies will have to deal with the combination of population growth ecosystem health, technology, and access to resources. Meeting the unmet need for family planning and reproductive health services should be part of national sustainable development strategies.

- The world needs to do a better job of forecasting the possible outcome of current human activities, including population trends, per capita resource-use, and wealth distribution.

Protecting the Atmosphere. The atmosphere is under increasing pressure from green house gases that threaten to change the climate and from chemicals that reduce the ozone layer. Governments need to:

- Modernize existing power system to gain energy efficiency and develop new and renewable energy sources.

- Promote national energy efficiency and emission standards and develop efficient, cost-effective, and less polluting mass transit systems.

Combating Deforestation. Forests worldwide are threatened by uncontrolled degradation and conversion to other uses because of increasing human pressure.

- There is an urgent need to conserve and plant forests in developed and developing countries to maintain or restore the ecological balance and to provide for human needs.
- Governments need to work with business, scientists, local community groups, indigenous people, and the public to create long-term conservation and management policies for every forest region and watershed.

Sustainable Agriculture and Rural Development. Hunger is already a constant threat to over 800 million people, while the world's ability to continue meeting growing demand for food and other agricultural products over the long term is uncertain. Soil erosion, salinisation, water-logging, and loss of soil fertility are increasing in all countries.

Agriculture has to meet rising needs mainly by increasing productivity, because most of the world's best croplands are already in use. At the same time further encroachment on land that is only marginally suitable for cultivation must be avoided.

- Sustainable agriculture and rural development will require major adjustments in agricultural, environmental, and economic policies in all countries and at the international level.

Conservation of Biological Diversity. The loss of the world's biological diversity continues, mainly from habitat destruction, over-harvesting, pollution, of foreign plants and animals (known and exotics). This decline in biodiversity is largely caused by human activity and represents a serious threat to our development.

- Develop national strategies to conserve and sustainably use biological diversity and to make these strategies part of overall national development efforts.

- Implement fair sharing of the benefits between providers and consumers of biological resources.

- Protect natural habitats. Promote the rehabilitation of damaged ecosystems.

Protecting and Managing the Oceans. Oceans are under increasing environmental stress from pollution overfishing, and degradation of coastlines and coral reefs. About 70 per cent of marine pollution comes from sources on land. Countries should commit themselves to control and reduce degradation of the marine environment. They should:

- Build and maintain sewage treatment systems and avoid discharging sewage near shell fisheries, water intakes and bathing areas.

- Develop land-use practices that reduce run-off of soil and wastes to rivers and thus to the seas. Use environmentally less harmful pesticides and fertilizers.

- Control and prevent coastal erosion and silting due to land uses such as unplanned construction.

Protecting and Managing Fresh Water. In many parts of the world there is widespread scarcity, gradual destruction, and increased pollution of fresh water resources. The causes include the inadequately treated sewage and industrial waste, loss of natural water catchment areas, deforestation and other chemicals into the water. The following approaches are key:

- The way to provide all people with potable water and basic sanitation is to adopt the approach "some for all rather than more for some." This approach can be achieved through low-cost services built and maintained at the community level.

- Nations need to identify and protect water resources and see that water is used on a sustainable basis. They need effective water pollution prevention and control programmes. There is a particular need for appropriate sanitation and waste—disposal technologies for low-income, high-density cities.

CHAPTER 16

One Battle After Another

Women fought for their rights throughout the twentieth century. In the past several decades, their struggles has truly become global, but all is far from won. We often hear that this will be century of women, in light of the tremendous strides that have been made in the past thirty years or so. Although it is far too soon to confirm this prediction, it can safely be asserted that the twentieth century was marked by their struggle to leave the home, where they were confined by the ancestral division of roles along gender lines. Around the world, women have campaigned to win the rights they have been denied and to build, side-by-side with men, the future of the planet.

True, such struggles had already been waged in the past, although they were deliberately shunned in official historical accounts. But the brief revolts of this special "minority", which accounts for over half of humanity, did not change the place of women in their societies. They may have ruled the roost, sometimes enjoying undeniable respect, but nevertheless they were still born to serve men and bring their husbands' descendants into the world.

Education: Their First Struggle

Yet, at the start of the twentieth century, the

traditional distribution of roles, seemingly legitimised by every religion and frozen in a "natural" order, began to crumble under the two-pronged assault of modernisation and women's struggle for their collective emancipation. They waged many battles to gradually obtain, despite set-backs, a change in their status—which is still far from achieved.

The first struggle of the twentieth century was for education. In 1861, a young woman graduated in Finance with a baccalaureate, a high school leaving examination, for the first time. In 1900, the first female university was founded in Japan. The same year, girls won the right to secondary education in Egypt and the first girl's school in Tunisia. Young women who could made the most of these new educational opportunities, not only to become better household managers and good educators for their children, as the main discourse of the period suggests, but also to do something unprecedented: to enter the forbidden spheres of public life, to exercise citizenship and to participate in politics. Throughout the twentieth century, women waged a battle on two fronts: by fighting for their own rights and taking part in the major social political emancipation movements.

The earliest feminist movements, which first appeared in the west in the late nineteenth century, focused on workplace and civil rights issues. Industry needed women's labour, which was underpaid in comparison with that of their male counterparts. 'Equal pay for equal work!' demanded American and European women, who began setting up their own trade unions and organizing strikes. They made unquestionable strides, but after more than one century of struggle, most women around the world still earn less pay for equal work.

The Right to Vote

The second objective of the twentieth century's pioneers was participation in public life, which hinged first and foremost on having the right to vote. The struggle was long and sometimes violent, as shown by the British "suffragettes" who demonstrated in the streets or Chinese women who made their demands heard by invading their country's new parliament in 1912. Everywhere, the fierce resistance of the political world progressively yieded to determined women's movements.

Control Over their Own Bodies

For a while, women's rights movements took a back seat to the Second World War and liberation struggles in the European colonies. The fight against fascism and, after 1945, colonialism, mobilised all their energy. Women distinguished themselves in these struggles, but that did not suffice to establish their rights as a gender. However, the world continued to change. With independence, many women in the South won access to schooling, salaried employment and, in a few exceptional cases, the closed world of politics. In Western countries, the post-war period saw them enter the workforce on a massive scale. The gap between social reality and the discriminatory laws defended by exclusively male power structures grew wider.

In the west, the second generation of feminists emerged in the wake of the libertarian movements of 1968. Picking up where their elders left off, they broadened the scope of their demands, for late-twentieth century feminists no longer aspired to the right to be "just like men" Challenging the claim of the "white male" to represent university, their goal was to achieve equality while remaining distinct as women. The women's liberation movement that first emerged in the American middle-class claimed the right to control one's own body. Feminists fought for contraception and abortion rights in many countries where one or both were against the law, and for autonomy and equality within the couple. "The personal is political", proclaimed women inspired by Marxism and psychoanalysis. "Workers of the world, who washes your socks?" chanted demonstrators in the streets of Paris in the 1970s. In France, the Veil Law legalizing abortion unleashed emotional debate in 1974.

Many Third World women could not identify with the struggles being waged in the West and insisted on leading their own battles at their own pace. However, these Western feminist movements breathed new life into the cause. Recognizing the changes and proclaiming their intention to accelerate them, the United Nations declared 1975 "International Women's Year" and organized the first international women's conference in Mexico City.

Already proclaimed in the Universal Declaration of Human Rights in 1948, sexual equality was reasserted in 1929 by the Convention on the Abolition of All Forms of Discrimination Against Women, which became a precious emancipation tool in the North as well as the South. At UN conferences in Copenhagen in 1980, Nairobi in 1985 and Beijing in 1995, women from both hemispheres found common ground, demanding the right to "have a child if I want it, when I want it," rejecting Malthusian principles and claiming their place in political bodies that until then had decided the world's future without them, struggling against religious fundamentalism that jeopardized their modest gains.

Misogyny of the Political Class

Of course, the struggle of Kuwaiti women against those who have denied that the right to vote or Indian women against the forced abortion of female foetuses is not the same as American women's battle against their own fundamentalists or French women's campaign against the misogyny take different approaches depending on the continent and do not necessarily have the same priorities, but the struggle has nonetheless become global during the past several decades. In the last twenty-five years, women have gradually increased their presence in public life, although it can hardly be said that the doors are wide open for them. From Africa to Asia, women's organisations have multiplied and acquired experience.

But their victories remain incomplete and the future is uncertain. From the nightmare of Afghan women to the ways in which equality is resisted in the so-called most advanced countries, the obstacles show that there is still a long way to go. Will women see the end of the struggle in this century that has just begun, the one which supposedly belongs to them?

CHAPTER 17

For a Fair Sharing of Time

Women may have entered public life on a massive scale, but they are still on their own when it comes to running the household. A new balance must be struck if there is to be genuine democracy. At the drawn of the 21st century, states and the international community can no longer refute the fact that humanity is made up of two sexes, not just one. This discovery, a precious legacy of the century that just closed, has brought women's existence into the limelight. One of the great democratic challenges for societies over the next century will be to mature so that both sexes are able to live their lives on an equal footing, with all their differences, contrasting history and culture, but also with equal rights and responsibilities.

Women's rise to power and their participation in politics are the vital signs of a healthy democracy. If only this vision that emerged from the 1995 Beijing Women's Conference could spread worldwide! one can call it a radicalisation of democracy. When women take part in the public arena, contributing to the ongoing, shared effort to shape better ways of living together, a qullitative leap occurs. Their participation fills a gap which has until now prevented the emergence of a truly democratic culture.

Archaic Attitudes

But attitudes are not the only obstacle to women's ambitions. The structure of society and the way men and women run their daily lives are other stumbling blocks. The Inter-American Development Bank has had the good idea of giving the Institute for Cultural Action, and NGO in Rio de Janeiro, the task of setting up a pilot programme to train women for positions of political and social power. Participants include trade union and NGO leaders, key figures from the black and indigenous communities, company executives, civil servants and policy-makers.

These women of different ages, educational backgrounds and ethnic origins are all aware of one fact: they are paying a very high price for a social contract that was negotiated when women were in a position of weakness, and agree that this has to change.

Remapping the Division between Public and Private Life

In Rio de Janeiro revealed that there is an urgent need to reorganize the use of time, to strike a new balance between responsibilities and to remap the division between public and private life. Household tasks must be recognised as time consuming, socially and economically vital and a serious check on women's ambitions.

Women in positions of power must constantly prove that they can behave like men. They keep quiet about having to look after children, run a household and care for elderly parents. Bringing those issues out into the open would mean admitting "flaws" that men do not have, for the simple reason that they delegate such work to their wives.

By drawing a veil of silence over their home life as if it were something illicit, women are allowing a basic fact to be hidden: the world of work relies on a domestic zone run by there. Women have changed, but the world of work has not and they are reaching the point of exhaustion. Filled with a deep sense of injustice, they are asking themselves: "Where did I go wrong?"

Understanding that humanity is composed of two different but equal sexes has several implications. Society must redefine itself because women are turning up in public carrying children in their arms and breast-feeding them, and because they have their own awareness and language that come from life experiences which are different from those of men.

An Untenable Double Burden

Articulating issues affecting public and private life is complicated, but that does not mean the equation is impossible of that the problems they raise should be brushed aside especially since the two worlds of public and private life are intertwined and mutually supportive. The balance between the two has now been upset. Women have entered public life on a massive scale, but the organisation of home life how time is used and who is responsible for what tasks is still the same, as if nothing had changed. And yet such a world, where women are expected to soldier on just as before, "simply" adding to their lives experiences hitherto reserved to men, is called egalitarian.

That misunderstanding is fueled by and age-old tradition of dismissing the world of women, even by women themselves. Because society does not consider what they do in the home as having any major social significance, it fails to add this part of their lives to the other side of the equation.

This is why the massive migration of women from the home to the public arena is occurring without societies having to think seriously about how and by whom domestic work will be done in the future (and which women still do, but at what cost!). The double burden, resulting from an out dated social contract, is putting women under mounting pressure by speeding up their lives to an untenable pace. We are facing a social problem that society as a whole must solve and not, as many think, a problem that women must settle by working even harder.

As new areas of power open up to women, both sexes must take a fresh look at how they use time. Rearranging it is a challenge to society's imagination. But has this necessity sunk into the minds of decision-makers? I do not think so. This poses a major problem because it is a missing building block in the construction of our democracies.

The everyday work is proof of this. Women must put these issues on the political and economic agenda, thereby contributing to a more radical definition of democracy. Feminism's new demand for a different sharing of time also opens a debate that goes beyond the interests of women alone. In the final analysis, time and its constants define the limits of our own lives and the range of choices we make, in accordance with the meaning we give to our own existence.

The equality equation is increasingly complex. It is not enough to wipe out the last traces of discrimination in public life. A new definition of equality will emerge when both sexes start sharing responsibility in the private realm. Otherwise, the issue will be distorted and women will lose all chance of succeeding in public life.

CHAPTER 18

Sex and Gender

A World of Difference

Understanding the differences between women and men, and how they are determined, is of key importance in understanding why a gender perspective is so important for development and the elimination of world poverty.

Differences between women and men are determined by biology, on the one hand, and society, on the other.

- Sex marks the distinction between women and men as result of the fundamental biological, physical and genetic difference between them.

- Gender roles are set by convention and other social, economic, political and cultural forces.

The precise boundary between these factors is the subject of fierce debate. Some people believe that the only important difference is that women can bear children and men cannot. Others believe that biology determines a much wider set of characteristics, attributes and capabilities. Whatever the case, the wide variation in the position of women in different societies around the world demonstrates that, unlike sex, gender roles are by no means fixed by nature—they are made by people, and can be renegotiated and changed.

The position of women in society is far from being of academic interest alone. It not only has fundamental consequences for the quality of life of both women and men, but also has a direct impact on a society's prosperity and well-being. The government's policy on international development recognises that gender-based inequality is a major obstacle to the escape from poverty. Studies have shown that developing countries which strive to ensure that women have equal rights have higher rates of economic growth, lower mortality rates, smaller and healthier families, and a better-educated population. Changing gender roles can make a world of difference.

The evidence also shows that gender equality is not luxury which can only be afforded by rich countries. UN data reveals that some developing countries outperform much richer ones in the opportunities they afford women. The better performing countries are scattered throughout the world showing that culture and religion need not be barriers to the advancement of women.

The gender gap in many countries is closing fast. Rapid progress has been made in recent decades. But in no society do women fare as well as men. Women are gaining ground in health and education terms, but still have a long way to go in sharing political and economic opportunities. They continue to suffer high levels of violence and abuse, and in many countries are treated differently to men by the law. These disadvantages are not due to sex differences, but are the result of gender discrimination.

Empowerment, Equality and Equity: What do they Mean?

Women's empowerment, gender equality and equity are key terms in debates about the changes required in the relationships between women and men.

- ***Empowerment*** means individuals acquiring the power to think and act freely, exercise choice, and to fulfil their potential as full and equal members of society.
- ***Equality*** means that women should have the same rights and entitlements as men to human, social, economic and cultural development, and equal voice in civil and political life. It does not mean that everyone should be the same, or that the benefits of development should be shared in exactly equal proportions by everyone. This would be neither feasible nor desirable, and would not be consistent with the notion of empowerment, which upholds everyone's right to determine their own future and the lifestyle of their choice.
- ***Equity*** means that the exercise of these rights should lead to outcomes which are fair and just, and which enable women to have the same power as men to define and pursue the objectives of development and shape societies of the future.

The difference between equality and equity is important because it underlines the rights of women to define the objectives of development for themselves and to seek outcomes which are not necessarily identical to those sought or enjoyed by men. Women have the right to pursue development paths which reflect their own needs and aspirations.

Upholding these rights is in the interests of men as well as women, because of the wider social and economic benefits brought by gender equality. Because of the universal disadvantages experienced by women, their empowerment is crucial to the achievement of equality and equity, the elimination of poverty and a better world for all.

CHAPTER 19

Gender-Based Violence

Around the world at least one woman in every three has been beaten, coerced into sex, or otherwise abused in her lifetime. Most often the abuser is a member of her own family. Increasingly, gender-based violence is recognised as a major public health concern and a violation of human rights.

The effects of violence can be deviating to a woman's reproductive health as well as to other aspects of her physical and mental well-being. In addition to causing injury, violence increases women's long-term risk of a number of other health problems, including chronic pain, physical disability, drug and alcohol abuse and depression. Women with a history of physical or sexual abuse are also at increased risk for unintended pregnancy, sexually transmitted infections and adverse pregnancy outcomes. Yet victims of violence who seek care from health professionals often have needs that providers do not recognise, do not ask about, and do not know how to address.

What is Gender-Based Violence?

Violence against women and girls includes physical, sexual, psychological and economic abuse. It is often known as "gender-based" violence because it evolved in part from women's subordinate status in society. Many cultures have beliefs, norms and social institutions that legitimise and therefore perpetuate violence against women. The same acts that would be punished if directed at an employer, a neighbour, or an acquaintance often go unchallenged when men direct them at women, especially within the family.

Two of the most common forms of violence against women are abuse by intimate male partners and coerced sex, whether it takes place in childhood, adolescence, or adulthood. Intimate partner abuse—also known as domestic violence, wife-beating and battering—is almost always accompanied by psychological abuse and in one-quarter to one-half of cases by forced sex as well. The majority of women who are abused by their partners are abused many times. In fact, atmosphere of terror often permeates abusive relationships.

How Health Care Providers can Help?

Health care providers can do much to help their clients who are victims of gender-based violence. Yet providers often miss opportunities to help by being unaware, indifferent, or judgemental. With training and support from health care systems, providers can do more to respond to the physical, emotional and security needs of abused women and girls.

First, health care providers can learn how to ask women about violence in ways that their clients find helpful. They can give women empathy and support. They can provide medical treatment, offer counselling, document injuries and refer their clients to legal assistance and support services.

Family planning and other reproductive health care providers have a particular responsibility to help because:

- Abuse has a major—although little recognised—impact on women's reproductive health and sexual well-being;
- Providers cannot do their jobs well unless they understand how violence and powerlessness affect

women's reproductive health and decision-making ability;

- Reproductive health care providers are strategically placed to help identify victims of violence and connect them with other community support services.

Providers can reassure women that violence is unacceptable and that no woman deserves to be beaten, sexually abused, or made to suffer emotionally.

Societal Responses

Health workers alone cannot transform the cultural, social and legal environment that gives rise to and condones widespread violence against women. Ending physical and sexual violence requires long-term commitment and strategies involving all parts of society. Many governments have committed themselves to overcoming violence against women by passing and enforcing laws that ensure women's legal rights and punish abusers. In addition, community-based strategies can focus on empowering women, reaching out to men and changing the beliefs and attitudes that permit abusive behaviour. Only when women gain their place as equal members of society will violence against women no longer be an invisible norm but, instead, a shocking aberration.

CHAPTER 20

Food First

By the time this day is over, about 40,000 human beings—mostly children—will have died from hunger, malnutrition and related causes. Today and everyday the deaths will mount, reaching an annual toll of 13 to 18 million. Few of these people will have been caught up in famine or other emergencies. Most will have suffered from a "silent" assault—the kind that seldom makes the headlines, but which claims its victims just as relentlessly.

It is intolerable that such deprivation and suffering should be allowed to exist in a world of potential food plenty. Having enough food is fundamental to all else. At the most basic level, this may entail humanitarian relief to assist people in emergency situations. In the transition from relief to development, however, we must look at systems for ensuring that societies have the capacity to produce or purchase the food they need and that it is accessible to all.

Sustainable food security fuses the goals of household food security and sustainable agriculture; it requires both. It requires looking not only at the aggregate supply of food, but also at the distribution of income and land, and at other issues: Do people have enough income to buy food? Enough land to grow their own food? Does the food distribution system deliver food where it is needed? How much food is wasted due to inadequate distribution systems? What are the implications of trends in population growth for future food needs? What is the status of women in society, and what opportunities do women have to alter rapid population growth rates? What is being done to regenerate the resource base for food production? These questions need to be asked and answered in every country.

The challenge of sustainable food security is immense, and it is growing. One billion people—20 per cent of the global population—are too poor to obtain enough food to sustain normal work. Half a billion are too poor to obtain the food needed for healthy growth of children and minimal activity of adults. Today's failure to feed people, however, may be but a prologue to a much larger failure in the future. Given likely population increases, world food output must triple over the next 50 years if the world's people are to have a nutritionally adequate diet. It will be difficult enough to achieve this expansion under favourable circumstances, and conditions may be far from favourable.

For example, according to recent estimates an area of about 1.2 billion hectares—the size of China and India combined—has experienced moderate to extreme soil deterioration since World War II as a result of human activities. Over three-fourths of that deterioration has occurred in the developing regions from causes such as overgrazing, deforestation, land clearing, unsound agricultural practices and increased soil salinity and water logging, largely from irrigation. Other environmental threats to the agricultural resource base include loss of water and genetic resources, adverse effects of pesticides and climate change, both local and global.

At the most aggregate level, the required increase in food production could be met if production grew at the historic average, that is, at the two per cent per annum rate achieved over the past half-century. But is this realistic? To produce three times more calories, all the land currently under cultivation around the world would, within 50 years, have to attain levels of productivity as high as those exhibited by the very best cropland today.

To this challenge add the possibility of diminished returns from the technological, energy and other inputs that have made agriculture so successful. Some experts believe that most of the potential for increased output of cereals—from improved plant varieties, from increased use of pesticides and fertilizers and from expanding the area under irrigation—has already been captured.

Viewed from this perspective, the goal of achieving sustainable food security in the decades ahead emerges as one of the greatest challenges humanity has ever faced. Agricultural output must be tripled, and people must have the income to buy the food they need. The erosion of the resource base must be halted and then reversed. Failure on any of these fronts will yield unprecedented human suffering.

What will it take to achieve sustainable food security? Obviously, the effort will have to be immense, both in size and complexity. Outlined below are a few simple (but no easy) steps that are absolutely essential elements of serious effort.

First, as citizens of the world, we must all come to see sustainable food security as a fundamental aspect of global peace and human security. This goes well beyond merely denouncing the use of food as a weapon.

Second, we must adopt concrete international goals, such as reducing world hunger by half over the next 10 years. We will never achieve the goal of sustainable food security unless we aim at specific milestones, and assess rigorously our progress in moving toward them.

Third, we must forge a true global partnership, a compact for sustainable food security. All countries—rich and poor—have important roles and responsibilities. There must be reciprocal responsibilities among nations, not one-way transfers.

Fourth, we must see deterioration of the agricultural resource base—terrestrial, aquatic and climatic—for what it is: a major threat to development and a major source of economic loss. Farmers are the largest group of environmental decision-makers in the world. We must ensure that they have the means to make sustainable development a reality where it counts—in the fields and fisheries.

Fifth, we must empower the people who work the land and who keep it productive. They are in the best position to decide the most appropriate ways to graft new technology onto their own traditional knowledge of seed selection, plant protection and nutrient-cycling. Special emphasis should be given to the role of women, the main providers for two-thirds of the poorest households in the developing world, as well as the producers of 60 per cent of all food grown and consumed locally.

Sixth, we must build the capacities of developing countries, both in government and in civil society. Capacity-building means empowerment for self-reliance. It means strengthening national capacities, both inside and outside government. This is essential for recognition and analysis of problems, for decision-making on courses of action and for management of systems and processes.

Seventh, not only must we build capacity in developing countries, we must also create linkages among researchers in industrial and developing countries. This will help minimize the time lag between discovery and practical utilisation. In addition, analysts from various countries must work together to examine future food security issues with different scenarios of population growth, agricultural productivity, markets and trade, climate change, loss of soil and bio-diversity and, last but not least, political instability, in order to devise options for rational choices.

We know a good deal about how to rid the world of the scourge of hunger, and how to begin to move toward sustainable food security on a global basis. We know that economic growth and prosperity are necessary, though not sufficient, conditions for eradicating hunger. We also know that developing efforts must encompass not only food production, but also socio-economic factors, including sustainable livelihoods for poor families, the implications of population growth rates, the status of women and girls and so forth. We also know that good words are not enough. Now more than ever before it is crucial that we marshal the political will to achieve our goals.

to meet growing developmental needs. On the other hand, to organise and manage development policies and programmes in a result-oriented manner, grows more difficult. The threat of further aid cuts and of further drops of public support for providing aid become ever more real. A closer look at the organisational complexities and political constraints under which development cooperation is expected to perform effectively may help to improve current aid management approaches.

Towards Conceptual Clarity

At first sight, catchy definitions of what constitutes effective aid might appear attractive to use, in particular with regard to economic indicators. The term "aid effectiveness" is easily used in the same vein as "efficiency", "significance" or "impact" of aid. At times, obsession to measure and demonstrate the results of aid supported development processes can be observed among policy-makers and administrators on the donor side. Still the understanding of aid and its effectiveness as being part and parcel of a cooperation relationship between donor and recipient side parties, is scarcely embedded in practice. To determine how to make aid more effective requires more than a quick impact analysis of an individual and perhaps even isolated development project. Consequently, defining the concept of aid effectiveness needs to take into account at what levels cooperation is focused on. To strive for sustainable and effective modes of development cooperation will entail the need to combine recipient ownership of the development process with donor accountability concerns.

Performance expectations cannot be exclusively placed on the recipient while donor interests, their aid management systems and procedures remain unchanged.

An extended and more analytical, process-oriented definition should take into account four main aspects of aid effectiveness:

(a) Effective aid must relate to the building and/or strengthening of in-country aid management capacity;

CHAPTER 21

Aid Effectiveness as a Multi-level Process

Parallel to the widespread decrease of aid resources provided by donor countries to developing countries in recent years, debate and research on how to make aid more effective has become a major concern. Usually, it is suggested that decades of development assistance have at best produced marginal results in terms of improving development levels in the South. Little mention is made of donor's policy shortcomings and the negative impact of these on efforts aimed at reforming and redefining development cooperation in order to enhance aid effectiveness. The policy parameters and operating frameworks of existing aid policies continue to inhibit higher degrees of aid effectiveness. In many donor countries, opinion polls indicate waning public support for development aid.

Increasingly, the moral case for aid is called into question and deeper world market integration tends to be seen as the panacea to continued economic decline and social destabilisation in the South. Against this background, cooperation between donor and recipient actors is faced with a duel uphill struggle. First, fewer resources can be mobilised (*b*) To maximise the degree of aid effectiveness, local ownership of the aid process is essential: from setting of priorities through policy formulation and implementation on to the evaluation stages of the process;

(*c*) Increasing recipient side capabilities to take charge of aid relationship, will need to be combined with arrangements to meet legitimate donor accountability concerns;

(*d*) Aid effectiveness is a two-faceted objective: its realisation is equally dependent on increased transparency of donor motives and on dropping of non-developmental, political and economic aid objectiveness of donors.

In addition a broader range of stakeholders in the aid relationship needs to be actively involved: extending beyond accountable government and implementing agencies, to include democratic institutions and organisations of civil society and of the private sector.

Applying any definition of aid effectiveness without disaggregating macro-economic data and taking into account country specificity will only lead to unhelpful generalisations about aid and its effectiveness. It would seem more appropriate to adopt working definitions against which to assess effectiveness of aid resources at a country-specific level. On such a basis one could expect to arrive at more reliable indicators of how well aid resources contribute to improving developmental standards and meeting existing needs.

From Definition to Success—Key Requirements

Having reached agreement between the recipient and donor on what should constitute effectiveness of aid is only a starting point. Embarking on democratic, peaceful and participatory patterns of economic and social development must follow: to arrive at significant and lasting improvement in many of the least developed countries will be a long-term process. This being said, it is crucial to design and implements such forms of development cooperation which involve a wide range of recipient side actors, not only from the government side but also from civil society at large. Seen as a process of increasing inclusion of intended beneficiaries of aid, the commitment to decentralise as well as entrust aid and its management grows in importance.

To fully capture Third World development realities, policy frameworks inspired by neoliberalist-type of development concepts and theories are grossly inadequate. The views and positions on aid articulated in the World Bank and the IMF, and others, represent only one side of today's international cooperation, namely the donor side. The major weakness to point out with respect to this locus of debate, is a profound under representation if not even a total absence of recipient experiences and perceptions on aid in general and on its effectiveness in particular. There should be little doubt that ignoring to not actively identifying and involving such perceptions, leads to strongly donor driven aid.

To circumvent recipient side insights and views on strengths and weaknesses of aid strategies and mechanisms, will result in limited local commitment and sense of ownership over the aid process. Mutual decision-making between donors and recipients remains a rare policy approach. Aid procedures that are based on local management and less control-oriented donor roles in the aid process are still exceptions in development cooperation.

Structurally, in terms of the policy environment within which development aid is expected to function, the overriding policy framework is general based on structural adjustment policies (SAP). But the underlying conclusion made by proponents of SAPs that these policies induce aid effectiveness, has yet to be proven valid. It must suffice at this point to emphasize that there is no *a priori* relationship between world market integration under structural adjustment and sustainable development in poor countries. Aid to these countries which is solely intended to reinforce fundamentally uneven and unequal patterns of world market integration should be scrutinised critically.

Some central issues need to be addressed in the course of improving aid and its effectiveness:

- institutional dimensions of aid relationships require strong policy-attention, both on the donor and the recipient side;
- capacities to effectively identify and formulate aid priorities need to be strengthened in recipient countries;
- local capacities to sustain reform efforts must be reinforced.

Levels of Intervention

If the design of aid and the terms upon which it is provided to a developing country are largely determined by the donor, the aid relationship can be characterised as essentially hierarchical. Recipient side views will rarely surface, as they are either not identified, or not well formulated. Possibilities of a recipient-led development strategies can be limited. Unless scope is provided to the recipient side actors to assume responsibilities, aid effectiveness is likely to remain low or fluctuating, and the sustainability of donor aid efforts will remain doubtful.

National planning processes and courses of national development in recipient countries should be seen as most effective where they are led under local responsibility and control. To arrive at this ideal situation, gaps need to be reduced and closed at the various intervention levels.

Donor aid resources provide valuable support for this process. Their effectiveness in meeting long-term objective of aid will need to be assessed on the basis of how well they perform at the different levels. Individual donors will expectedly perform differently at the various levels. What will prove to be the ultimate test for effectiveness is how well the donor aid performance accomplishes the broader objectives of development cooperation and how well it includes sustainable results.

In the analytical frameworks outlined here, development cooperation would seem to be confronted with the effectiveness gaps at the:

- *Structural Level:* International trade and investment patterns, debt problems and world market integration process appear as long-term constraining factors upon aid and its effectiveness;
- *Policy Level:* Dialogue and partnership in development cooperation are instrumental factors in recluding planning and co-ordination gaps with regard to policy analysis and formulation;
- *The Institutional Level* is where pertinent capacity gaps exist: capacity development efforts of donors and technical assistance measures play an important role in addressing weaknesses in aid effectiveness within a country's institutional setting;
- Finally, at the *level of aid projects* (programmes), it is generally the lack of sustainability of aid interventions which causes development activities to falter once donor support decreases or stops. In addition to technical cooperation, financial and material inputs serve to maintain project momentum and goal realisation. The issue of how to develop local capacity sufficiently in order for indigenous organisations to continue project activities initially supported by donor aid, remains the most important issue to address at this level.

Fostering Aid Effectiveness

In recent years donor aid budgets have been reshuffled, while having decreased in real terms. Geographical redistributions of reduced aid budgets have been accompanied by the need to accommodate rising emergency needs.

Additional resources to meet these needs have not been forthcoming: in general, aid budgets destined for developmental purposes have been under severe pressures while urgent humanitarian needs have added to the drain on resources.

Donor and recipient development efforts are too often isolated from one another, or poorly coordinated. They fail to address managerial and implementation bottlenecks. Cross-sectorial linkages, as well as interdisciplinary approaches to aid problems are only slowly gaining ground. It is increasingly obvious, that decisions on aid issues are subjected to concerns outside of the responsible ministry: Finance Ministers, Economics Ministers and unfortunately even Defence Ministers have a strong say in how much aid is to be provided, where it is to be concentrated and under what terms to be utilised. Inside of recipient countries, large portions of national budgets are allocated to non-development priorities with little or no impact on alleviating urgent poverty problems.

Development cooperation may make the biggest impact and be executed most effectively where donors and recipients agree upon multi-level aid strategies. To give an example, building a road to a remote rural area may well be done in an effective project manner. It is equally important to have a functioning transport authority in place to ensure maintenance of the roads. If this authority operates within a nationally defined infrastructure policy, best in accord with national trade and investment priorities, then the effectiveness of the project-level road building programme has a good chance of being high.

Institutional changes to set the stage for a profound reform process in development cooperation are needed. Reprioritising national budgets to reflect identified in country development needs may be one step. Setting up policy evaluation and formulation units can be complimentary measures. Deregulating markets and investment rules may serve to please donors, but dumping of cheap products which strangle local production efforts may easily result. Regional cooperation, including intensified South-South cooperation can provide some counterbalance. There are only a few areas where changes in the current system of development cooperation can occur, with a view to better manage the complexities of aid and the social, cultural, economic and political backgrounds against which they take place. The will and commitment to take policy action in both donor and recipient countries, through the broadest range of stakeholders and institutions as possible, will be the test for genuine efforts at improving development relations between North and South and organising cooperation effectively.

CHAPTER 22

The Status of Saving

National saving rates have been declining for several years in many countries of the industrial and developing world. Given the importance of saving to the global economy, this trends is causing much concern. Saving is critical to maintain growth and to help solve the problem of international debt. Declining saving rates have been associated with lower rates of capital accumulation and slower growth in the global economy. Moreover, differing rates of saving among countries have contributed to the emergence of large trade imbalances.

Most economies agree that if these long-run trends continue, they would have a serious impact on international economic growth. Yet attention has recently shifted to the potential consequences of a more immediate threat—that of a short-run global capital shortage. There are claims that this is caused by increase demands on global financial resources resulting from such events as the process of transition in Eastern Europe and the former Soviet Union, German unification, reconstruction of the Middle East, disaster relief, and structural support of countries in debt. At the same time, large private and public sector deficits persist in important industrial countries. Even countries like

Germany and Japan are experiencing a decline in their traditional surpluses of capital because of structural changes in their economies.

These factors mean that world capital markets are likely to become increasingly competitive. Countries needing capital in both North and South may face scarcer supplies of funds. Can the perceived shortage of global savings be avoided? Do the world's financial markets have the capacity to absorb additional demands for funds? Can structural changes in the global economy take place in the global economy take place in a way that does not jeopardize growth? Or, will a savings shortage perpetuate high interest rates (or even increase them) and limit economic growth?

Trends in Saving

Global savings and investment are notoriously difficult to measure. The latest reliable estimate puts total world saving at approximately US $5.2 trillion in 1995. On a global scale, both saving and investment have declined as a percentage of the gross national product (GNP) since the early 1980s.

Since the mid-1980s, the OECD countries have become net importers of capital. All over the world, and particularly in North America and a few other industrial countries, government debt generates a demand for money. OPEC countries provided most of the financial resources needed by world markets during the 1980s. But since the downturn in oil prices hit the OPEC region in 1983s, newly industrialising countries in Asia (and particularly Taiwan) have largely take over this role. About 80 per cent of total private saving is accumulated in the industrial world. In the developing world, Africa has consistently suffered from insufficient saving, although the situation has improved slightly during the 1980s. More recently, Asian and Latin American countries have become excess savers.

Global Balance

For an individual country, or even a region, imbalances

between savings and investment are not necessarily critical. A country can invest more that it saves and borrow what it needs on capital markets. Countries that are excess savers supply the necessary funds. On a global scale, however, the supply of savings must equal the demand for investment. In other words, one country's investment must be another country's savings.

But the global balance between planned saving and desired investment can be lopsided. For example, greater demands for investment will trigger processes of adjustment; either the price of borrowing capital will rise (i.e., higher interest rates) or certain investment projects will not be funded. Capital shortages largely affect world markets through higher interest rates. Indeed, world interests rates did rise during the 1980s and the early 1990s. The 1980s have in fact been quite a typical, in that real (meaning corrected for inflation) interest rates have persisted at unprecedented levels. Possibly as a result of greater demands on world financial markets. Competing economic theories have identified a number of potential culprits for this enduring increase. An insufficient amount of savings (either current or expected) is only one of many hypotheses explaining the rise in real interest rates.

Reduced Demand

The unification of Germany, the transitional economies of Eastern Europe and the Commonwealth of Independent States, reconstruction of the Middle East, and new lending to developing countries account for about a 3 per cent increase in demand for world savings. There are, however, trends in other areas that appear to signal a reduced need for funds. For example, investment has slowed in the previously booming commercial real estate markets in the United States and elsewhere. Moreover, there are indications that the rates of fixed investment in Japan during the 1980s are not likely to be sustained.

The possibility also exists for more savings in the public sector industrial countries. These range from prospects for tax increases in Germany to massive reductions in military expenditures, particularly in the US. The rapid advancement of European integration is likely to lead to improved fiscal discipline and consolidated budgets, and thus reduced public sector spending. At any rate, government deficits are still critical and reducing them will be important for future national saving in industrial countries.

Private saving behaviour is difficult to project in that it reflects as society's values and changing preferences. The latest medium-term International Monetary Fund forecast, however, show that private savings in industrial countries will drop by about 0.5 per cent of GNP, primarily because of a rapidly aging population and the corresponding increase in the ratio of dependents to wage earners in Japan and many European countries.

Although world saving might be insufficient over the short- and medium-term, it is also evident that even small changes in the current economic environment and in public and private sector behaviour could generate enough funds to eliminate the problem entirely. A first conclusion is, therefore, that forecasts of a major saving gap or an imminent capital shortfall should be treated with some sceptism. Consequently, concerns that insufficient saving will lead to increases in world real interest rates are also mostly unwarranted.

Credit Squeeze

Claims on world financial resources are likely to squeeze the amount of capital available from multilateral development banks and bilateral institutions to many small developing countries. This rationing of financial support may be as important for this group of countries as the potential eroding of the favourable terms of international lending. Small adjustments to the level of support can translate into significant setbacks for the most vulnerable countries.

Any globally co-ordinate scheme to give financial aid to selected regions must include safeguards so that the smallest, least developed, and highly indebted countries still have access to the finite sources of capital available to international agencies.

Why should individual countries be concerned about the global supply of funds, when, in the long-run, growth for any country is financed out of domestic saving? There is little evidence to suggest that the degree of access to external funds effects medium-term growth rates in developing countries. In fact, during the last two decades, economic growth was generally lower in the developing countries that borrowed than in those that did not. This was largely due to the high interest rates of the 1980s suffered by severely indebted countries. Even earlier, however, borrowers' growth rates were only marginally higher than those of non-borrowers. Although the borrowed funds helped boost per capita income, it is less likely that they stimulated the economies of the recipient countries. Differences in the developing countries' growth have largely been the result of differences in their rates of domestic saving. Form this perspective, national saving should be encouraged.

Fears Unfounded

A tentative conclusion is that fears or a global capital shortage, skyrocketing real interest rates, and negative effects resulting from greater demands on international financial resources over the next few years are most likely unfounded. There appears to be as many trends pointing toward increases in saving as there are indications of additional capital needs. Also, even if substantial savings shortfalls were to materialise, the limited rise in real interest rates would have relatively benign effects on countries of both North and South. The only major caveat relates to small developing countries that have in the past depended upon favourable terms of lending from multi- and bilateral institutions. If international capital shortages translate into even the smallest encroachment on the allocation of funds to these countries, their medium-term development could be threatened. In addition, the debt burdens of many developing countries suggest that in the long-run, external sources of funds cannot substitute for sufficient national saving. If domestic saving correspondents to development needs in the South, developing countries should not suffer as a result of increased competition for international capital.

Finally, while the short-term fears of a global capital shortage are clearly unwarranted, concerns about the medium-term trends in world saving are not. National saving rates must be raised substantially throughout the world to allow real interest rates to decline to the post-war average of 1 to 1.5 per cent. That, more than anything else, will contribute to a stable expansion of the global economy.

CHAPTER 23

India's Food Challenge

Is India's population growing disproportionately to its food supply? Will famine once again hit millions of people? Most agriculture experts agree that a Malthusian crisis is not likely to occur in the near term. The reason; the overall food situation in India has been characterized by a large increase in regional output since the famine-ravaged 1960s.

At that time, the food situation was described as "desperate" in India. Famine had plagued India's Bihar state in the sixties. International food specialists predicted further famine because food production looked as if it would lag for behind population growth. Instead, average crop yields per acre soared, thanks to the introduction of high-yielding varieties of rice and wheat and to expanded irrigation and chemical fertilizer use. It has been called the "Green Revolution".

Double Role of Irrigation

The keys to the higher food production have been irrigation, the adoption of high-yielding varieties (HYVs) of foodgrains and the increased use of modern inputs such as fertilizers. Irrigation has played a double role, it has not only helped raise yields through synergistic interaction with

HYVs and fertilizers, but has also contributed to considerable increases in harvested area by enabling higher cropping intensity.

Still, there are ominous clouds on Indian food horizon. In light of the region's high population growth, increased urban sprawl and rampant environmental degradation, there are signs that hunger problems could loom unless action is taken by Indian's and international development agencies.

Shrinking Base

The favourable food supply situation is likely to disappear within the next decade, due to a shrinking resource base. The earlier decades had witnessed a natural resources based growth strategy as there was adequate land and water resources for development. But this is fast disappearing due to urbanisation, industrialisation and ecological degradation. We should also remember that about 50 per cent of food production is from rainfed lands and a few years of drought could alter the food security which we now enjoy. The high costs of irrigation and land development, coupled with low commodity prices, are also hampering required investments and these effects will be seen in the next decade.

By the year 2030, India will have to produce 60 per cent more rice with much fewer resources. Clearly, there will be a major challenge for scientists and policy-makers to meet the increased food demand. India's population is growing 2 per cent a year, making the challenges for regional food security a daunting task.

The solution for meeting future food demand will be breakthroughs in science and technology since yield levels have reached a plateau and are even showing signs of decline. The possibilities through biotechnology and genetic engineering are exciting and can herald another "green revolution". This is the only hope for avoiding the Malthusian dilemma.

In gauging the region's population-food squeeze, it is useful to look first at its swelling population. India—the world's second populous region contains several states with high population growth rates.

Ironic Problem

Rapid population growth dilutes and impedes economic development. An increase in the population base puts greater pressure on finite resources, both financial and natural, and, in the context, worsening of income distribution, increased poverty incidence and environmental degradation.

Moreover, there is the ironic problem, that although rapid population growth increases poverty, poverty encourages larger families through its impact on access to education and decreased prospects for child survival.

If population growth is uncontrolled, the economic and social consequences are:

- ecological imbalance, with greater pressure on natural resources;
- increased urban crowding, with increases in demand for municipal services and infrastructure;
- a more unequal income distribution, particularly as labour supply outpaces job creation;
- signs of mass poverty, including high infant and child mortality rates, high levels of child malnutrition and hunger, poor school performance, unemployment and underemployment.

Bleak Prospects

Existing population growth rate is unsustainable, even for the relatively near future. Unless population growth rate is kept within manageable limits, the prospects for creating acceptable standards of living for low-income groups in India will be bleak.

The Indian population is growing more rapidly than ever before and will continue to do so for at least four decades. Indeed, without major technological breakthroughs and changes in patterns of consumption, even the most optimistic population growth projections are likely to be accompanied by increase in poverty, hunger and environmental degradation.

Whether we look at population, the environment or development, the next 10 years will be critical for our future. The decisions we make or don't take will widen or narrow our options for a century to come. They could decide the fate of the earth as a home for human beings.

CHAPTER 24

Consuming the Future

Now that we are to reach six billion of us, it is a good point to check again on what sort of lifestyles we pursue and what is the environmental impact of those lifestyles. It is curious that we have spent several decades being concerned about the growing numbers of humankind while not giving at least an equal amount of attention to the levels of living we aspire to, and how many natural resources we chew up thereby and how much pollution and waste we cause.

Everybody is a consumer of sorts. True, every fifth person scarcely qualifies for that designation, consuming goods worth less than $1 per day. Conversely, every seventh person qualifies for a designation of super-consumer, with a cash income at least fifty times greater. These latter are the people who, through their carbon dioxide emissions, are disrupting everybody's climate dozens of times more than the average citizen of One Earth. Fair play, anyone?

Much as the have-nots seek to match the have's, it is plain their efforts will not work out for a long time to come, at best. If every Chinese person were to consume just one additional chicken per year and if the said chicken were to be raised primarily on grain, this would account for as much grain per year as all the grain exports of the number two exporter, Canada. If the Chinese were to raise their per capita consumption of beef, now only 4 kgs per year, to that of Americans, 45 kg, and if the additional beef were produced largely in feedlots after the manner of the United States, it would account for as much extra grain as the entire US grain harvest, less than one-third of which is exported. Because of its recent climbing up the food chain toward a meat-based diet, China has become one of the world's leading importers of grain. The global grain market today is around 200 million tons per year, and shows scant scope for significant increase.

As a further measure of its ambitions, the Chinese government has designated the auto industry as one of five industry "pillars". Today China has fewer cars than Los Angeles. If per capita car ownership, together with oil consumption, were to match that of the United States, China would need 80 million barrels of oil per day—by contrast with the world's 1996 oil output of 64 million barrels of oil per day. The surge in carbon dioxide emissions would be unprecedented.

All this notwithstanding, there are already some 250 million newly affluent people in China. They are people with a household income equivalent to perhaps US $20,000, and enough discretionary income to enjoy the perquisites of the good life as perceived by these nouveaux riches. Top of the shopping lists are meat and more meat, followed by cars whether big or small. These are the badges of success: they show you have arrived.

The new consumers in China are matched by at least 200 million in India, and tens of millions in South Korea, Taiwan, Malaysia and Thailand (the recent economic setbacks have not permanently punctured the economic bubbles). Then there are 200 million more in Brazil, Argentina, Venezuela and Mexico, and more again in Hungary and other countries of Eastern Europe, also Turkey. Put them all together and they total about as many as the 800 million long established consumers in the ultra rich countries (the OECD grouping). When the current economic hiccups in Asia are left behind, the ranks of the new consumers can be expected to rise rapidly.

But they cannot hope to become super consumers. Where would all the extra gain come from? How could the global climate tolerate the huge additional pulse of carbon dioxide? There are all kinds of other environmental reasons to suppose that environmental constraints will become all the more constraining. True, technology could help moderate the environmental impact. We could enjoy twice as much material prosperity while using only half as much natural resources and causing half as much pollution and waste. But the new consumers will want to pursue the American dream to the hilt, and it is hard to see that the best technologies could enable huge numbers of affluent aspirants, perhaps two billion people by 2010, enjoying even half the material prosperity of Americans with average household incomes of $40,000.

But is it true "prosperity"—mental and emotional as well as material? Or is the American dream becoming a nightmare with its harried lifestyles and declining leisure time, where the shopping mall is the ultimate mecca, and the good life is a case of piling up goodies?

In any case, we cannot expect the new consumers to forego their "rightful share" of affluence unless the long-time affluent agree to cut back on their environmental ruinous lifestyles. It is these communities that must offer a strong example, and soonest. Where is the political leader who will espouse the new vision, however much it may be perceived as the ultimate vote loser?

CHAPTER 25

The Environment, The Economy and Public Health
An Integrated View

The environment is central to the health of people and their economies. Just as a foetus is totally dependent on the life-support system of the mother during her pregnancy, so the health and vitality of people and their economies are totally dependent on their environments. Unfortunately, many people do not see it that way. They either see the environment as dependent on the economy—such as the politician who says: "let's make the economy strong, then we'll fix the environment when we can afford it"—or they see little connection between health and the environment, whether they are "deep greens" campaigning on ecological issues or doctors treating individual patients and individual illnesses. Whether we are politicians, greens or doctors, is there not a more efficient way to fulfil our aims? For this, a broader perspective is essential.

All economies are sub-systems of the larger environmental system which provides the:

- sources of energy and materials;
- sinks for pollution and other wastes;

- services of water, nutrients and carbon recycling;
- space for living, working and aesthetics ("a walk in the woods and the song of a bird").

Neglect of this life-support system of the "4 S's" leads to weaker or defunct economies as vegetation, food, soils, water or air become contaminated or exhausted and gradually fail to support economic activity. This is dramatically illustrated in the Aral Sea region, or the collapsed Canadian salmon fishing communities.

Indirect Social Costs

Less catastrophic but still costly is where economic damage is caused by pesticides and nutrient contamination of groundwater, involving millions of Rupees in water treatment. This is a social cost to the economy that the agricultural sector does not include in the price of its food: an economic distortion that reduces the real wealth of society via false price signals that encourage the over-use of pesticides and fertilisers. Similarly, the "external" costs on society of road-respiratory-induced accidents, noise, respiratory and circulatory diseases and congestion amount to a lot of money to any government but these costs are not borne by transport users, which mean that transport is encouraged beyond the level that is economic for society as a whole. By internalising these externalities via taxes and other means, the market prices for transport would become fairer and more efficient. Currently only about 30 per cent of transport externalities are covered by transport taxes. But if the health of an economy is dependent on the health of its environment, what about the health of its people?

Without access to the basics of clean water, shelter, fresh air and food, people obviously suffer. Even in more developed economies where the link between everyday life and the environment is not so visible, the role of environmental factors in disease and well-being is significant. Most of the major diseases such as heart disease, cancer, respiratory diseases and allergies have an environmental as well as a genetic component within a multi-factorial chain of causation. And while each environmental factor may be small, if the links in the chain of causation are inter-dependent, as they often appear to be then removing even a small link can break the chain.

Environmental Factors

Take asthma in children, for example. These seem to be many causes, from a child's genetic inheritance to its nutritional status, which in turn help determine how it reacts to the many environmental factors, both indoor (such as mites, pets, damp, environmental tobacco smoke, nitrogen oxides) and outdoor (such as pollen and pollution from industry and traffic), that have been implicated in asthma causation. Therefore it is clear that diagnoses of asthma and many other diseases should systematically embrace environmental factors. This will be a significant challenge for doctors whose time is scarce and whose training is not usually appropriate.

This multi-causal chain will vary in its exact make-up from child to child, but for children overall, even if the evironmental factors such as damp housing to traffic fumes may be less important than, say, genetic make-up or nutritional status, the environmental factors may be the ones that can be most cost effectively removed, thus breaking the causal chain. And, as with many environmental issues, there are secondary benefits of action, such as less noise or fewer accidents from traffic reduction, or energy savings from dry houses, which further justify the environmental actions even where exact causations are not well understood.

The environmental causes of disease and ill-health are a controversial and ill-understood area of science and opinions vary about their significance. Some say that, for Western Europe, perhaps 2-3 per cent of public disease and ill-health is determined by known environmental factors but others maintain that it must be far more significant. They point to the sharp increase over the last two or three decades in asthma, allergies, and cancers (particularly of the reproductive organs such as breast and testicles) and related ill-health such as sperm count decline, which cannot be explained by genetic causes. They also observe that the large differences in health between the socio-economic classes cannot be explained without involving significant environmental causation.

It is thought that the ubiquitous presence of low doses of mixtures of chemicals in food, drink, air, consumer products and the general environment are playing some role in public ill-health, even if the evidence for this is far from substantial.

Impact on Public Health

But what about environmental programmes and campaigns being little concerned with health? Well, history so far shows that the environment only gets serious attention when it is seen to be damaging either the economy or public health. Yet because "everything connects" in "socio-enviro" systems, action to stop infectious diseases from water contamination, or to reduce skin cancer from ozone depletion, leads to a better environment for all species. And if upland forests are preserved because they are seen to be cheaper and more effective water regulators (which reduce the risk of lowland flooding) than dams, then upland biodiversity benefits anyway, even if it was last in the queue for political attention.

Although public health may be seen by some as only a small part of "the environment", much environmental progress depends upon the political weight of the health impacts. For example, the cost benefit exercise on the current multi-pollutant/effect programme on acidification, eutrophication and low-level ozone shows that it is the benefits to human health, not eco-system damage, that provide the main economic justification for further reductions in SO_2, NO_x and NH_3. Ecologists need the language of public health in order to maximise political support for the environment. So, it is out of our specialist "boxes" of economics, health and ecology, and into a shared systems approach, with integrated programmes that build partnerships for progress.

CHAPTER 26

Development Requires More Ownership

To achieve lasting economic growth and a substantial reduction in poverty, developing country ownership needs to be successively strengthened. The international debate on what constitutes the right economic policy for development has become considerably more intense in recent years. Some of the recommendations that prevailed in the 1980s and 1990s, based on neoclassical economic theory, had to be revised. Central to the economic recommendations of the 'old' Washington Consensus were liberalisation and deregulation of the economy as well as 'neutral' monetary and fiscal policies.

With the Cologne debt relief initiative the Washington consensus and its structural adjustment strategy were basically relegated to the past. They were superseded by the concept of Poverty Reduction Strategy Papers (PRSPs). This approach depends on developing countries drafting policies themselves ("ownership") with the involvement of civil society ("participation"). So far, however, the international financial institutions have neither thought to the new concepts through to their conclusion nor placed them in a coherent context. Several conceptual gaps still remain.

It is still largely unclear how forces can be mobilised for growth in developing and transition countries and how their economies might be better shielded against external shocks and instability. In the light of current trends, it is feared that many countries will hardly achieve the Millennium Development Goals (MDGs) unless sustainable economic growth is attained and harnessed to reduce poverty.

This suggests that donors have not adequately implemented the new approaches yet. While the Bretton Woods institutions have introduced sweeping reforms—the World Bank has acknowledge the key role institutions and "governance" play in development and has replaced its purely market based approach in favour if more practical solutions—discrepancies between vision and reality persist on the ground.

Shortcomings of the Washington Consensus

Some of the shortcomings of the old policy recommendations are well known. They ignored distribution issues, for example, paid little attention to the role of institutions, and assigned only a passive role to macro-economic management. The neoclassical equilibrium model on which the Washington Consensus is based permits analysis of allocation aspects but does not take institutional or socio-economic structures into account. The "Standard Packages" of structural adjustment programmes were usually far less differentiated than the related political recommendations in general. Core elements of the programmes were swift privatisation and liberalisation of capital markets. Deregulation and liberalisation were deemed adequate requirements for optimising resource allocation and paving the way for high growth.

Efficient institutions curb insecurity and thus increase readiness to invest. Long-term maintenance of dynamic growth processes is possible only where there are institutions, which help boost productivity, guarantee a high degree of stability and reduce vulnerability to external shocks.

Unconventional Approaches

Such findings need to be properly thought through and translated into action. This means actively helping developing and transition countries to plot their own course. It also follows from the paradigm shift marked by PRSP that donors should accept unconventional policy measures. "Ownership" means donor institutions, should open to alternative economic policy options, including macro-economic options. Without diversity at concept level it will not be possible to mobilise sources of growth on the requisite scale.

The discussion paper makes a number of general conclusions: relating to economic policy. They particularly concern the quality of institutions, regulatory systems and governance and the issue of property rights, which needed to be seen as factors fundamental to all other forces for growth. These issues should systematically be taken into account when economic reforms are drafted. This is especially true for reforms based on liberalisation and privatisation. If necessary, liberalising action should be postponed until the minimal requirements are met in institutional and macroeconomic terms. The question of time frames for reform should also be given serious consideration and not as is often the case-dismissed as a mere detail of "timing and sequencing".

There is no universal recipe for development. Solutions need to be customised and country- specific. It is important that reforms should be anchored in the political, economic and cultural landscape of the developing country in question and that its financial and administrative capacities ought to be taken account of. Feasible reform needs to be given higher priority then ideology. Second-best or even third-best options are generally better than "pure doctrine" if they suit the context of the country.

More attention needs to be paid to the question of dept sustainability Financial transfers—and especially Overseas Development Agency (ODA) loans—need to result in more investment and higher productivity. Situations where countries amass unsustainable mountains of debt need to be prevented to reduce susceptibility to external shocks. ODA should take account of individual countries' situations. This calls for more flexible, more adequately tailored financing instrument For MICs, the structure of external debt is also significant: short-term volatile currency transfers are particularly problematical.

Confining Conditionality

To increase long-term growth and to substantially reduce poverty. developing country owership needs to be successively strengthened. Primary requirements are:

- better use and targeted development of local analytical capacities (for instance through Poverty and Social Impact Analyses—PSIAs);
- advice by external partners (especially the Bretton Woods institutions) on a wide range of policy options including unconventional policy proposals;
- no taboos concerning macroeconomic issues; they should be included in the PRSP process; and
- geater cofinement of world Bank and IMF programme conditionalities to core areas.

Better safeguards should be provided against external shocks. The lending policy of multilateral and bilateral donors needs to be adjusted to suit the debt sustainability of recipient countries in this context, it is important to (continue to) develop financing facilities, which allow swift assistance in the event of external shocks. At the same time, financing instruments need to be designed to reduce debt-servicing risks. Examples could be government bonds with interest payment tied to GDP growth or more flexible arrangement for the servicing of concessionary credit. To eliminate exchange rate risks. More ODA loans should be denominated in local currencies.

The World Bank needs to strengthen its strategies for crisis prevention and, in particular, for dealing with external shocks and managing crises.

More account needs to be taken of macro/micro-level interaction. Efficient strategies for promoting economic growth and reducing poverty are possible only where macro and micro-policies are functionally interwoven.

Last but not least, PRSP processes need to be improved and poverty reduction and other development strategies made more explicit. It is a well-known fact that many PRSPs do not adequately define priorities, identify trade-offs between the different goals and measures or signal the budgetary implications of the measures that are planned. In particular, they generally fail to make any mention of potential sources of future economic growth, let alone craft strategy for mobilising them. Only when these shortcomings are eliminated can PRSPs become real planning tools.

CHAPTER 27

Peace and Poverty

Peace should not be understood in military terms, like absence of armed conflicts. Peace should be understood in a human way in a broad social, political and economic way. Peace should mean social justice between nations and within nations. It should mean establishment of human rights for all people.

In the new context the concept of "peace" would be the existence of a political and economic environment where each individual human being is truly free; free from the control of any powerful person or any powerful nation, free from poverty, hunger and indignities, each individual human being free to explore the limits of one's own potential.

Today peace is threatened, more than anything else, by poverty, unjust social and economic order, absence of democracy and environmental degradation.

The cold war cloud has gone. You can feel the breath of fresh air around the world. Now there is no visible competitor left for capitalism. It is quite risky to live with a philosophy, which has no challenger. To be safe, we must go to the essence of the philosophy of capitalism rather than be satisfied with the practices, which emerged over years through patchworks of expediency.

Contrary to common belief, it is not the "free enterprise" which is the essence of capitalism. It is the freedom of individual thought and freedom of individual action which is the essence of capitalism. It is these freedoms, which support free enterprise, free trade, free circulation of capital, and free circulation of people.

We must work out a new system, appropriate for the new world, from the basics of capitalism, not from the practices of capitalism. Many of these practices take away freedom, rather than guarantee it. Traps must go. People cannot remain trapped in places where they cannot live because of ecological, political, or economic reasons. This planet belongs to all people. If some people are trapped somewhere, we must all come forward to remove the causes of their discomfort. At the same time we must leave our shores open for anybody who decides to join us, or anybody who decides to part our company.

Poverty denies a person control over his destiny. Poverty means not being able to tell what tomorrow would be like. If we examine the situation carefully we'll see that the poverty is neither created by the poor, nor sustained by the poor. It is the system of policies and institutions that we have built around us that creates and sustains poverty. Poverty is the denial of human rights. Over one billion people live below the absolute poverty line right now on this planet, are denied of almost all human rights. There is no way one can defend the existence of poverty anywhere. Poverty is a disgrace for the entire mankind. Because we allow another human being to die of hunger, or malnutrition, or common curable diseases, or exposure to climate, we are reduced to less human being. If a particular world system is responsible for creating this massive poverty we must act to replace it.

Resource-wise or technology-wise, there is no reason why poverty should exist and continue to deepen and widen. If we make up our minds to wipe out poverty from the surface of the earth, the worst aspect of poverty can be removed within the next couple of decades.

We can build a poverty-free world at a fraction of the cost of what we spend on war preparations. Nations become very generous when it comes to making their war-machine heftier in the name of ensuring "peace". Can we persuade ourselves to allocate a part of our time, money and intellect to achieve peace by making the people at the bottom the winners, rather than nations winning wars? "Peace" achieved by winning wars is earned by destroying people. The real peace can be achieved by building people, by reinforcing people, by helping people to reach their potential. Removing poverty is the process of building people.

Each human being is a wonderful creation of the creator. Each human being is born with great potentials. Poverty denies any opportunity for a person to achieve any of his/her potential. We have built a world system, which is in the habit of pushing people down not building them up. It creates barriers around individuals, rather than remove them.

The most effective step that we must take to remove poverty is to create a system, which creates enabling conditions for people and removes the existing barriers. The institutional barriers were skilfully crafted over the centuries to benefit a handful of people.

Resource-poor nations with high incidence of poverty waste away enormous human capability each day by denying poor people the use of their energy and ingenuity. If they could have been made economically active, not only they could have contributed in the national production, they would have helped expand the domestic market for the products produced. The poor can be transformed into the engine of growth if we only allow them to unleash their capacity.

We cannot be at peace with ourselves if we know there is a human being who lives a life worse than an animal. A human being is supposed to live differently than an animal.

He/she is supposed to live a life with human dignity. Human dignity is what distinguishes a human being from an animal. When we cannot ensure this dignity for others, our own dignity becomes an empty pretence.

There must be a thousand and one ways to remove poverty from the earth. We may or may not know some of those ways already. Obviously there are many more ways yet to be designed, each more effectively than others. When we shall find them, how many of them we shall find, how quickly we find them; will depend on how eager we are to find them. But to say that poverty cannot be overcome, directly and quickly, is to underestimate the capacity of human mind.

Poverty is homogeneous only when considered from the point of view of income or consumption: the uniformity of the poor as a category exists only on the level of the fact that they have little to consume. When considered from the point of view of production, i.e., the circumstances in which the poor must operate to gain their income, the conditions of poverty are extraordinary diverse. A concrete grasp of these diverse circumstances is the first step in developing relevant instruments to address not only the problems of the poor, but also the challenge of taking advantage of the opportunities available to them.

The conventional means of measuring economic progress, such as Gross National Product per capita, tell us little about the real nature of poverty. In recent years this sort of yardstick has been supplemented by measurements of food security, income distribution, and social development (encompassing health and education). These offer the possibility of composite indices, allowing the development of more rounded characterisations and comparisons of poverty at the national level. However, these principally refer to the symptoms of poverty, not to the relational factors generating it. Poverty is not a state of being; it is the effect of dynamic processes. While it is important to know where poverty is greatest, it is critical to know why it exists. This inquiry necessarily leads away from the nature of the poor as individuals to the nature of their social and physical environment. Poverty is not only a personal phenomenon, it is a social status. As such, while its effects can be measured on the level of the individual, its causes must be sought elsewhere. From the point of view of poverty alleviation the process of becoming is just as important as the state of being.

At the heart of poverty is the inadequate access of the poor to productive resources. Low incomes tends to reflect inadequate means of production, not incompetent producers. However, poverty in India is not simply a reflection of private resources. A broad range of "external" factors impinge on incomes, among them the following:

National Policies

One of the ironies of Indian development is that while no government wants poverty, many policies contribute to it—what is given in anti-poverty programmes is drained away by other policies. The poor do not always come out ahead in the balance—they are often net "donors" to the rest of society. Frequent reference is made to unsustainable forms of development—to urban over-expansion, industrialisation based on subsidies, and to public sector engorgement. What is less frequently realised is that the bill for these phenomena is often presented to the rural poor. Taxation of exports to sustain sectors with little export potential of their own and subsidised food imports to supply the urban population are policies that are often paid for by the rural poor. In many areas of India, exports are agricultural goods produced by small farmers. Here export taxes contribute to rural poverty. The same is true of "cheap" food imports, which depress the prices paid to small farmers for their food crops.

"Structural imbalance" is not only a recipe for increasing external indebtedness; it is also a recipe for increasing the poverty of the rural population. The political weakness of the poor in most areas is not only the basis for inadequate poverty alleviation programmes and policies—it is the basis for an actual transfer of their income to more socially influential groups. While it is often correctly asserted that the poor are the first to suffer from adjustments involving public social expenditure cuts, it is often the case that they also have the most to gain from the elimination of policy-based economic distortions that reflect social power rather than productive efficiency and potential.

Demographic Factors

Accelerated population growth is a long-term contributor to poverty. In India the incomes of the poor have declined, mortality rates are also falling, pushing the numbers up. In the meantime, land is becoming scarcer, plots more fragmented and the soil and pasture increasingly degraded. This phenomenon is not without its policy dimensions. As long as the poor remain undercapitalised, and essential determinant of household income is the amount of labour available to its household economic strategies favour large families. While population policy has a role to play, possibly more critical is a change in the economic environment. Access to capital and more secure income changes perceptions of the need for labour. In the medium- and long-term, population dynamics are driven by the underlying productive systems. As long as the production systems of the poor remain underdeveloped, population growth remains high, restricting even the future possibility of development.

Natural Resource Management and the Environment

If poverty is both cause and effect of rapid population expansion, so poverty is both cause and effect of many dimensions of degradation of the environment. Many of the rural poor, but by no means all, live in areas of extreme environmental fragility, a circumstance often prompted by high level of control by the better-off over more stable and productive resource areas. Here the poor are extraordinarily exposed to the dangers of erosion, whittling away at an already meager productive base. The threat is not entirely due to nature. Rather, poverty accelerates erosion. Without capital, the poor are frequently unable to invest in even traditional methods of soil and water conservation. And without sufficient land they are forced to shorten fallow periods, putting further strain on the resource base. As in the case of population growth, the result is strain not only on the poor, but on the entire Indian economy. Given the extremely limited economic alternatives, the solution to this problem is not to forbid the use of environmentally fragile resources to the poor; it is to change the conditions under which their use takes place. Access to conservation technology is important; but more so are security of land tenure and resources to invest.

Combating poverty means not only increasing the production of the poor, but also preserving and enhancing the long-term value of the resource they control. What this very often means, in practice is assisting the poor in reestablishing a stable relationship with fragile resource. Prevailing processes in many areas involve the gradual—and sometimes not so gradual—depletion of natural resources, to the detriment of all. Part of the answer to this is conservation. Part of the answer is also to provide viable economic alternatives to the poor, reducing their dependence on erosion-prone crop and livestock practices.

Exploitative Intermediates

The poor are not unaware of the pressure upon them, and also of means of overcoming them. Their ability to respond, however, is severely impaired by social powerlessness. The poor are surrounded by a dense network of public and private factors reducing their freedom of action, and actually draining what few resources they do have. Members of the network include traders and moneylenders capitalising upon the economic weakness of the poor, and engaging them in unequal exchanges. They also include public agencies either indifferent to the requirements of the socially uninfluential, or actively engaged in extracting "surplus" for use by other groups. Not to be excluded from this are organisations which are ostensibly "for" the poor, but which, in fact, serve as systems of containment and control.

Bibliography

BOOKS

Awasti, D.S. *Role of Women in Economic Development,* Kanpur, Indian Economic Association.

Awadi, S.K. *Economic and Planning in Retrospect,* Vikas Publishing House Pvt. Ltd., New Delhi, 1983.

Ahluwalia Montck, S. (1985), *Rural Poverty Agricultural Production and Prices: A Reexamination* in John Mellor and Desai Gunvant, M. (eds.), *Agricultural Changes and Mural Poverty,* The John Hopkins University Press, London.

Appadorai, A. *Status of Women in South Asia,* Orient Languages Ltd., Calcutta, 1954.

Asthana Prathima, *Women's Moment in India,* Vikas Publishing House, New Delhi, 1974.

Ajit Mazumdas, *Problems of Unemployment in India,* 1997.

Ashok, K. Arora, *Financing of Small-Scale Industries,* Deep & Deep Publications, 1992.

Ashok Mitra, Lalit Pathak, Shekar Mukherji, *The Status of Women Shifts in Occupational Participation,* Abhinav Publications, 1980.

Arun Kumar, *"Social Characteristics of Working Women,"* Sarup and Sons Publishers, New Delhi.

Beard, Mary, R., *Women as force in History: A Study in Traditions and Realities,* The Macmillan Company, New York, 1946.

Boser Up, E. *Women's Role in Economic Development,* George Allen, London, 1970.

Bela Rani Sharma and Raj Pusti, *Encyclopedia of Women Society and Culture Series—Post-Independence India and Women,* Anmol Publications Private Ltd., New Delhi.

Betellei, A., *Chronicles of Overtime,* Penguin Books, New Delhi, 2000.

Chakaravarthy Sukamay, *Development Planning: The Indian Experience,* Oxford University Press, New Delhi, 1989.

Charsely, S.R. and G.K. Karanth, *Challenging Untouchability, Dalit Initiative and Experience from Karnataka,* Sage Publications, New Delhi, 1998.

Carr, Mary et al., *Speaking Out, Women's Economic Empowerment in South Asia,* Vikas Publications, New Delhi.

Dantwala, M.L., *Dilemmas of Growth: The Indian Experience,* Sagar Publications, New Delhi, 1996.

Desai, Deera, *Women in Modern India,* Vora Anand Company, Bombay, 1959.

Desai, A.P., *Essays on Modernization of Underdeveloped Society,* Thzekar and Company Limited, Vol. I & II, 1971.

Dinakar Rao, K., *Women's Development: Linkages for Credit,* New Delhi.

Desai, B.M. and N.V. Namboodiri, *Rural Financial Institutions: Promotion and Performance,* Oxford and IBH Publishing Company Pvt. Ltd., New Delhi.

Desai, S.S.M., *Rural Banking in India,* Himalaya Publishing House, Bombay, 1983.

Delige, R., *The Untouchables of India,* Berg, New York, 1999.

Dev, S. Mahendra, *State Interventions and Women's Employment,* in T.S. Papola and Alakh N. Sharma (eds),

Gender and Employment in India," Vikas Publishing House Pvt. Ltd., New Delhi, 1999.

Dharm Narain and Sen, A.K. et al., *Studies on Indian Agriculture,* Oxford University Press, New Delhi, 1989.

Engles, E., *The Origin of the Family, Private Property and State,* Reprinted by Progress Publishers, Marlow, 1994.

Frencine Fournier, *Foreword, Poverty and Participation in Civil Society,* Edited by Yogesh Atal of Else Oyen, Abhinav Publications, New Delhi, 1997.

Gandhi, M.K., *To the Women,* Anand T. Hingorani, Karachi, Bharatiya Vidya Bhavan, Bombay.

Gandhi, M.K., *Role of Women and Social Justice,* Navjeevan Publishing House, Ahmedabad, 1958.

Gunner Myrdal, "Economic Theory and Underdeveloped Regions," Vora and Company, Bombay, 1958.

Gunner Myrdal, *Asian Drama—An Enquiry into Poverty of Nations,* Pantheon, New York.

Gunner Myrdal, *The Challenge of World Poverty: A World Anti-Poverty Programme in Outline,* Pantheon, New York, 1970.

Ghosh, S.K., "Women in a Changing Society," Ashish Publishing House, New Delhi, 1984.

Gupta, D., *Interrogating Caste: Understanding Hierarchy and Difference in Indian Society,* Penguin Books, New Delhi, 2000.

Griffin, *The Political Economy of Agrarian Change,* The Macmillan Press Ltd., London, 1979.

Griffin Keith, *International Inequality and National Poverty,* The Macmillan Press Ltd., London, 1978.

Griffin Keith, *Land Concentration and Rural Poverty,* The Macmillan Press Ltd., Hong Kong, 1981.

Haleh Afshar, *Women, Work and Ideology in the Third World,* Tavistock Pup, London & New York, 1985.

Hathi, J.L., *Problems of Unemployment in India,* 1974.

Harper, M. *Profit for, the Poor,* Oxford and IBH Publishing Co., Delhi, 1998.

Haq, Mahabub Ul, *The Poverty Curtain: Choices for the Third World,* Oxford University Press, Bombay, 1978.

Haq, Mahabub Ul, *Human Development in South Asia,* Oxford University Press, New York, 1997.

Heggade, Odeyar, D., *Women and Economic Development: A Study of the Different Facets of their role in India,* Ramya Roopa Prakashan, Bangalore, 1984.

Holcombe, Susan, *Managing to Empower: The Grameen Bank's Experience of Poverty Alleviation,* Oxford University Press, Dhaka, 1995.

IFMR, *An Economic Assessment of Poverty Eradication and Rural Unemployment Alleviation Programme and their Prospects,* Madras, 1984.

Jackson Dudley, *Poverty, Macmillan Studies in Economics,* Macmillan, London, 1972.

Jain Devaki, *Indian Women,* Ministry of Information and Broadcasting, Government of India, 1975.

Jawaharlal Nehru, *Women of India,* The Director, Publications Division, Ministry of Information and Broadcasting, Government of India, Delhi, 1958.

Jaya Kumar G. Stanley, *Status of Women in Male Dominated Society,* ISSR Publishers, Vellore, 1992.

Kamatha Prasad, *Planning for Poverty Alleviation,* Publishing Academy 208, Defence Colony, New Delhi.

Kalbagh, C, *Women in Enterprise and Profession,* Discovery Publishing House, New Delhi.

Karmakar, K.G. *Rural Credit and Self-help Groups, Micro-Finance Needs and Concepts in India,* Sage Publications, New Delhi, 1999.

Lalitha, N., *Rural Women: Empowerment and Development Banking,* Kaniska Publishers, New Delhi.

Kaushik Dasu, *The Development Economy: A Critique of Contemporary Theory,* Oxford University Press, Delhi, 1984.

Kuznets, S., *Economic Growth and Structure,* Heinemann, London, 1965.

Lewis, A., *Development Planning,* Allen & Unwin, London, 1966.

Mahajan, V.S., *Women's Contribution to India's Economic and Social Development,* Deep & Deep Publications, New Delhi.

Maheswari, S.R., *Rural Development in India,* Sage Publications, Delhi, 1985.

Minhas, R.S., *Planning and the Poor,* S. Chand & Company Limited, New Delhi, 1974.

Mukta Mittal, *Women Power in India,* Anmol Publications Pvt. Ltd., New Delhi, 1995.

Myrdal Gunner, *Asian Drama,* Volume III, Twentieth Century Fund, 1 New York, 1968.

Manohar and Murali, *Socio-economic Status of Indian Women,* Seema Publications, Delhi, 1983.

Murthy, S. & Gaur, K.D., *Women Work Participation and Empowerment: Problems and Prospects,* RBSA Publishers, Jaipur.

NABARD, *NABARD and Micro-Finance,* Mumbai, 1999-2000.

NCERT, *Human Development in South India,* Oxford, New Delhi, 2000.

Nanda, Y.C., *Role of Banks in Rural Development in the New Millennium, National Bank for Agriculture and Rural Development,* Mumbai, 2000.

Padmini Sen Gupta, *Women in India,* Information Services of India, New Delhi, 1964.

Pandya, B.A., *Women Organizations and Development,* Illustrated Books Publishers, Jaipur, 1994.

Parthasarathy, G., *Integrated Rural Development Concepts: Theoretical Base and Contradiction in Development Planning and Policy,* edited by Gupta, D.B., et al., Wiley Eastern, New Delhi, 1982.

Pigou, A.C., *The Economics of Welfare,* Macmillan & Co. Ltd., London, 1960

Rai and Tandon, *Voluntary Development Organisation and Socio-Economic Development,* Indian Economic Association, 82nd Conference Volume, Amritsar, 1999.

Romy Borooah, *An Interdisciplinary Look at Women, Households and Development,* edited by Romy Borooah and Others," Sage Publications, New Delhi, 1994.

Sapru, R.K., *Women and Development,* Ashish Publication, New Delhi, 1989.

Sahai, *Women in a Changing Society,* Mittal Publications, New Delhi, 1985.

Sakuntala Narasimhan, *Empowering Women: An Alternative for Strategy from Rural India,* Sage Publications, New Delhi, 1999.

Sen, A.K., *Poverty and Famines: An Essay on Entitlement and Deprivation,* Oxford University Press, Delhi, 1984.

Todaro Michael, P., *Economics for a Developing World,* Second Edition, Longman, New York.

Tokli, M.R. & Sharma, D.P., *Rural Banking in India,* Oxford & IBH Publishing Company, New Delhi.

Thakur, R.N., Education and Political Status of Indian Women: Key to Economic Development, *Women and Economic Development,* A. Banerjee & R.K. Sen (ed). 2000.

United Nations Development Fund for *Women—An End to Debt: Operational Guidelines for Credit Projects,* UNLHEM, New York, 1993.

Venkata Reddy, K., *Rural Development in India,* Himalaya Publishing House, Bombay, 1988.

Vasanth Desai, *Indian Banking Nature and Problems,* Himalaya Publishing House, Bombay.

Von Pischke J.D. et al., *Rural Financial Markets in Developing Countries: Their Use and Abuse*, John Hopkins University, Baltimore, USA, 1983.

Yogesh Atal, *Poverty and Participation in Civil Society,* Abhinav Publications, New Delhi.

Zweig, F., *Women's Life and Labour,* Victor Gollanz, London, 1952.

JOURNALS

Aggarwal, P., Role of Women in Socio-Economic Development," *Social Walfare,* March, 1987.

Aziz Wahida, 'The Place of Women in National Life,' *Social Welfare,* Vol. IX, No. 24, March 23, 1945.

Awasthi, P.K. et al., 'IRDP: Receptivity and Reaction,' *Indian Journal of Agricultural Economics,* Vol. 41, No. 4, October-December.

Arunachalam Jaya and Azad Nandini, 'Role of Women and Children in the Informal Sector,' Productivity, 26 (3), 1985 (Oct-Dec.).

Aggarwal, Deepti, 'Empowerment of Rural Women,' *Intensive Agriculture* 39(1-2), 2001 (March-April), pp. 3-5.

Amod Kumar, 'Towards Women's Empowerment: The Equation of Education and Economics,' *Women's Link,* 6(3), 2000 (Jul-Sept.), pp. 15-19.

Azim, Shaukath, 'Gender Empowerment: Where does India Stand?' *Social Welfare,* 48(2), 2001 (May), pp. 9-11.

Bark B.B. and Vannan, P.P, 'Promoting Self-Help Groups: As Sub-System of Credit Cooperatives,' *Coopcrator,* 38(7) 2001 January, pp. 305-12.

Berger, Marguerite, 'Giving Women Credit: The Strengthens and Limitations of Credit as a Tool for Alternating Poverty,' *World Development,* 17(7), 1989 July.

Behra, L., 'Success Story: Self Help Groups in Sati (Orissa) Making Rapid Progress,' *Cooperator,* 34(1), July 18, 1996.

Bagchee Sandeep, 'Poverty Alleviation Programmes in Seventh Plan: An Appraisal,' *Economic and Political Weekly,* Vol. XXII, No. 4, January 24, 1987.

Bardhan, P.K., 'On the Incidence of Poverty in Rural India of the Sixties,' *Economic and Political Weekly,* February 1973.

Kulkarni, D., Vijaya, 'Empowerment of Women through Self-Help Groups,' *JANATA*, 56(23), 2001 (Aug.), pp. 12-15.

Kulshrestha, R., Laxmi and Gupta, Archana, 'Self-Help Groups: Innovations in Financing the Poor,' *Kurukshetra,* 2001 (Nov.), pp. 26-29.

Kumaran, K.P., 'Self-Help Groups: An Alternative to Institutional Credit to the Poor: Case Study in Andhra Pradesh,' *Journal of Rural Development,* 16(3), 1997 (July-Sept.), pp. 515-30.

Kalpagam, U., 'Women, Informal Sector and Perspectives on Struggles,' *Social Scientist,* 15(6), 1987 (June), pp. 33-44.

Kabir, M., 'Participation of Women in Cooperative Programmes, Economic Activity, Social Change and Family Planning,' Social Action, 37(2), 1987 (April-June), pp. 163-73.

Kumar Rajinder, et al., 'Impact of Credit on Income Employment and Capital Formulation of Rural Poor,' *Indian Journal of* Agricultural Economics, Vol. 41, No. 4, Oct-Dec. 1986.

Kullur, M.S., 'Empowerment of Women through NGOs: A Case Study of MYRADA Self-Help Groups,' *Indian Journal of Agricultural Economics,* Vol. 41, No. 4, Oct-Dec. 2001.

Lakshmikanthan, K.R., 'Sell-Help Groups in the Life of Rural Floor: A Pilibhit Case Study,' *Women's Link,* 6(2), 2000 (Apr-June), pp. 10-16.

Launch of Certificate Programme on Empowering Women through Self-Help Groups, *Social Welfare,* 47(7), 2000 (Oct.), pp. 30-31.

Levy, Leon, H., 'Self-Help Groups: 'Types and Psychological Processes,' *Journal of Applied Behavioural Science,* 12(3), 1996 (July, Aug-Sep.), pp. 310-322.

Lokayan, 'Workshop on Empowerment of Women in Household Space,' *Women's Link,* 6(4), 2000 (Oct-Dec.), pp. 46-48.

Mohanan, S., 'Micro Credit and Empowerment of Women—Role of NGOs,' *Yojana,* 44(2), 2000 (Feb.), pp. 21-23.

Lalit Kumar Tyagi, 'Poverty Eradication through Self Help Promotion,' *IASSI Quarterly,* Vol. 18, No. 1, 1999.

Murugan, K.R. and Dharmalingam, 13, 'Self-Help Groups: New Women's Movement in Tamil Nadu,' Social *Welfare,* 47(5), 2000 (Aug.), pp. 9-12.

Madeley, John, 'Hill Women of Nepal take the Credit,' *Development and Cooperation,* 4, 1991, pp. 16-17.

Mohammadi, Pari, 'Women in National Planning: False Expectations,' *Development,* 4, 1984, pp. 80-81.

Mohiuddin, Asghari and others, 'Evaluation of preparedness status of state governments for implementation of DWCRA Programme in the field,' *National Bank News Review,* 4(1), 1988 (March), pp. 29-32.

Marina Rinta, 'Development through Empowerment of Women in India,' *Kurukshetra,* August, 1995.

Narayan Reddy, G, 'Integrated Approach to Women's Development and Health Delivery Systems in Rural Areas, NIRD Experiences,' *Journal of Rural Development,* September, 1992.

Naib, V.P., 'Self-Help Groups in Rural Development,' *Panchayat Aur Insan,* 6&7 (12&1), 1995 (March & April), pp. 5-6.

Nanda, Y.C., 'Linking Banks and Self-Help Groups in India and the role of NGOs: Lessons learned and future perspectives,' *National Bank News Review,* 15(3), 1999 (Jul-Sep), pp. 1-9.

Narayanswamy, R. and Roy, A.K., 'Women Empowerment through Cooperatives: A Case Study of Mahila Vikasa in Andhra Pradesh,' *Cooperative Perspective,* 34(5), 2000 (Jan-Mar.), pp. 63-68.

Ojha, R.K. 'Self-Help Groups and Rural Employment,' *Yojana,* 45(5), 2001 (May), pp. 20-23.

Owusu, K., Opoku and William Tetteh, 'An Experiment in Agricultural Credit: The Small Farmer Group Lending Programme in Ghana,' *Savings and Development,* Vol. 1, No. 1, 1982.

Patel, I.G., 'Promotion of Credit to Women Entrepreneurs,' *Reserve Bank of Indian Bulletin,* 1981. Dec. 35(12), pp. 1059-64.

Patel, A.R., 'Entrepreneurship and Small Business Development for Women,' *Kurukshetra,* August, 1995.

Rajeswari, G. and Manimekalai, N., 'Empowerment of Women through Self-Help Groups (SHGs), *Margin,* 32(4), 2000 (Jul-Sept.), pp. 74-87.

Ramesh, Ashwini, 'Self-H$_e$lp Groups and Small Village Co-operatives for Rural Development: A Critical Perspective Vision,' *Indian Cooperative Review,* 18(1), 2000 (July), pp. 30-37.

Ramesh, Ashwini, 'Why Self-Help Groups and Why not the Village Cooperatives for Rural Development: A Critical Perspective Vision,' *Cooperative Perspective,* 35(3), 2000 (Oct.-Dec.), pp. 30-35.

Rani, T. Usha and Others, 'Role of Women in Dairy Development—A Case Study,' *Yojana,* 35(16), 1991 (Sep.15), p. 26.

Role of Women Central to Population and Development Issues, *Asian-Pacific Population Programme News,* 11 (1&2), 1982 (Quarterly), pp. 11-13.

Ranjan Kackar, 'DWCRA—Andhra Women March Towards Employment,' *Gramin Vikas Newsletter,* July, 1995.

Raka Gupta and Bipin Kumar Gupta, 'Role of Women in Economic Development,' *Yojana,* August, 1987.

Rajaram Das Gupta, 'Working and Impact of Rural Self-Help Groups and other forms of Micro Financing,' *Indian Journal of Agricultural Economics,* Vol. 56, No. 3, 2001.

Satyanarayana Reddy and Renuka, 'DWCRA: A Boon for Rural Women,' *Yojana,* 1994 December.

Sadeque, Syed, 'The Rural Financial Market and the Grameen Bank Project in Bangladesh an experiment in involving poor and women in institutional credit operations,' *Savings and Development,* 2, 1986, pp. 181-96.

Sivaram Reddy, C., 'Development of Women and Children in Rural Areas—An Appraisal,' *Kurukshetra,* 1988, February.

Scheyvens, Regina and Leslie, Helen, 'Gender, Ethics and Empowerment: Dilemmas of Development Fieldwork,'

Women's Studies International Forum, 23(1), 2000 (Jan-Feb.), pp. 119-30.

Sengupta Milanjan, 'Empowerment: A Socio-psychological approach to Self Help Group Formation,' *Prajnan,* 26(4), 1998 (Jan.-March), pp. 523-34.

Sharma, S.L., 'Empowerment Without Antagonism: A Case for Reformulation of Women's Empowerment Approach,' *Sociology Bulletin,* 49(1), 2000 (March): 19-40.

Singh Mor, D.P., "Issues and Initiatives in Women's Empowerment," *Social Welfare,* 48(6), 2001 (Sep.), pp. 22-27

Singh, J.P., "Indian Democracy and Empowerment of Women," *Indian Journal of Public Administration,* 46(4) 2000 (Oct.-Dec.), pp. 601-16.

Singh Sukhpal, "Self Help Groups in Indian Agribusiness: Reflections from Case Studies," *Artha Vijnana,* 37(4), 1995 (Dec.), pp. 380-88.

Srinivasan, N., "Why *Self' Help Groups:* Borrower's Point of View," *National Bank News Review,* 12(1), 1996 (Jan.-Mar.), pp. 18-19.

Suguna, B., "Women's Empowerment: Concept and Framework," *Social Welfare,* 48(9) 2001 (Dec.), pp. 3-7.

Surikanthi A., "Literacy: Essential for *SHG's," Social Welfare,* 47(6), 2000 (Sep.), pp. 32-34.

Saibaba G., "Pattern and Problem of Women Employment," *Eastern Economist,* Vol. 65, No. 1, July 4 No. 1 and 2, 1975, New Delhi.

Thakurela, S.K., "DWCRA and Credit for Women," *Gramin Vikas News Letters,* 1993 (Oct.-Nov.).

Tyagi, Ombeer Singh, "Women's Empowerment: A Micro Perspective, *Women's Link,* 6(1), 2000 (Jan.-Mar.), pp. 37-39.

Thakur, D.S., 'Rural Development in India: Past Experience and Tasks Ahead,' *Indian Journal of Agricultural Economics,* Vol. XXXII, No. 3, July-Sep. 1977.

Uma Joshi, 'Rural Women: A more Purposeful Role', *Kurukshetra,* August 1997, p. 94.

Verma, G.L., "Women Beneficiaries and IRDP,' *Journal of Rural Development,* 1986, July.

Vajpaye, A.B., Women's Empowerment Year "Give Women the Freedom of Choice," Social *Welfare,* 47(11), 2001 (Feb.), pp. 5-12.

Venkata Ravi and Venkataramana, M., 'Self-Help among Scheduled Caste *Women, Indian Economic Panorama,* 9(4), 2000 (Jan.), pp. 36-42.

Venkata Subramanian, K., "Women Empowerment,' *University News,* 39(42), 2001 (Oct.), pp. 14-17.

Viswanathan, K.S., 'Self-Help Groups—Their Role in Irrigation Development and Management,' *National Bank News Review,* 81 (11-12) 1993 (Jan.-Feb.), pp. 36-37.

Wickrama K.A.A. and Keith, Pat. M., 'Savings and Credit: Womens' Informal Groups as Model for Change in Developing Countries,' *Journal of Developing Areas,* 1994 April.

Wadhwa, Subhash, C., "Self Help Groups for Reaching the Poor," *Financing Agriculture,* 27(3), 1995 (July-Sep.), pp. 4-12.

Yaron. J., "Successful Rural Finance Institutions. World Bank Discussion paper, 150, Washington, D.C. USA, 1997.

REPORTS

APDPIP, on Andhra Pradesh, District Poverty Initiatives Project Appraisal Document (PAD), Report No. 20089 South Asia Regional Office, 2000.

Chief Planning Officer, Handbook of Statistics, 1993-94, Kurnool District.

CIRDAP, Increased Household Income and Rural Women in Asia, Impact on Status and Activities, Dhaka, Bangladesh, 1998.

CIRDAP, Poverty, Gender and Participation, Dhaka, 1998.

CIRDAP, Rural Development Report, Center on Integrated Rural Development for Asia and Pacific, Dhaka, 1999.

Government of Andhra Pradesh, Annual Report of the Commission of the Rural Development, Hyderabad, 1998.

Government of Andhra Pradesh, Annual Report of the Commission of the Rural Development, Hyderabad, 1999.

Government of Andhra Pradesh, Provisional Population Totals, Series 29, Hyderabad, 2001.

Government of Andhra Pradesh, Statistical Abstract, Hyderabad, 2001.

Government of India, Census of India, Registrar General, New Delhi, India, 1991.

Government of India, Seventh Five Year Plan, New Delhi, 1985-90.

Government of India, Eighth Five Year Plan, New Delhi, 1990-95.

Government of India, Ninth Five Year Plan, New Delhi, 1997-2002.

Government of India, Provisional Population Totals, New Delhi, 2001.

Government of India, Towards Equality Committee on the status of Women in India, 1974.

Government of India, Tenth Five Year Plan, Planning Commission, New Delhi, 2002-07.

Government of Andhra Pradesh, Vision-2020, Hyderabad, India, 1999.

Government of Andhra Pradesh, Strategy Paper, 2001.

IFAD, The State of World Poverty, Rome for a Discussion on the Process and Structural Causes of Poverty, see Rovert Chambers (1983), Rural Development, Putting the Last First, London, Longmans one of the Best Discussions on how these Perpetuate Poverty, 1996.

IFAD, "Rural Poverty Report, The Challenge of Ending Rural Poverty," Oxford, Ford, New York, 2001.

International Fund for Agricultural Development (IFAD), "The State World Rural Poverty—An Inquiry into its Causes and Consequences", New York University Press, New York.

NABARD, Annual Report, Mumbai, 1999.

NABARD, Annual Report, Mumbai, 2000.

NABARD, Annual Report, Mumbai, 2001.

NIRD, Rural Development Report; Rural Employment, Hyderabad, Andhra Pradesh, 1994.

NIRD, National Conference on SHG Movement in the Country & Swarnajayanti Gram Swarozgar Yojana (SGSY), National Institute of Rural Development, Hyderabad, Andhra Pradesh, 2001.

South Asian Association for Regional Cooperation (SAARC), The Independent Source Asian Commissions of the SAARC on Poverty Alleviation, Dhaka, 1992.

South Asian Association for Regional Cooperation (SAARC), Meeting the Challenge, Report of the Independent South Asian Commission on Poverty, 1992.

The World Bank, World Development Report, Oxford, New York, 1990.

The World Bank, Gender and Poverty in India, Washington DC, 1991.

The World Bank, World Development Report, 1999-2000, Oxford University Press, New York.

The Hindu, April 27, Chennai, 2002.

The Hindu, Vision-2020, 2002.

UNDP, Human Development Report, Oxford, New York, 1994.

UNDP, Human Development Report, Oxford, New York, 1996.

UNDP, Human Development Report, Oxford, New York, 1997.

UNDP, Human Development Report, Oxford, New York, 2000.

OTHERS

Government of India, Report of the Committee on the Status of Women in India, Ministry of Education and Social Welfare, New Delhi, 1974.

Government of India, Fourth World Conference on Women, Beijing, 1995, Country Report, Department of Women and Child Development, Ministry of Human Resources Development.

APDPIP, on Andhra Pradesh District Poverty Initiatives Project Appraisal Document (PAD), Report No. 20089, South Asia, Regional Office, 2000.

Index

D

E

F

G

H

I

L

M

N

O

P